D1538679

MEMORIES

Desmond MacCarthy

MEMORIES

FOREWORDS BY
RAYMOND MORTIMER
&
CYRIL CONNOLLY

New York

OXFORD UNIVERSITY PRESS

1953

First published in 1953

*Printed in Great Britain
by Robert Cunningham and Sons Ltd.
Alva, Scotland*

FOREWORD

by RAYMOND MORTIMER

WHEN Desmond MacCarthy died, we lost the best of contemporary critics. If this judgment seems coloured by my gratitude and affection, let me ask what other writer in our time has responded to such a variety of work with an appreciation at once so discriminating and so infectious? His books take up only a small space on our shelves: except for a slight volume dealing with the Court Theatre, all his work was done for periodicals, and is now easily accessible only in the selections made by his friend Pearsall Smith, and later by Lady MacCarthy and Mr James MacGibbon. If, however, an academic writer condemns it for this reason as journalism, he should similarly dismiss the greater part of Addison and Hazlitt.

Desmond MacCarthy was sincerely over-modest in judging his work: it was so much slighter than what in his youth he had dreamt of achieving, slighter too than what with his extraordinary gifts he might have achieved. Nor was this due chiefly, I think, to his having to earn a livelihood; I should say rather that his gusto for life kept him from the ascetic regularity and solitude that authorship usually demands. He preferred reading to writing—so as a rule do all but the worst writers; to add that he preferred talking to reading might be excessive, but I have never known anyone who more enjoyed talking, or who talked better. In any case, the laziness with which he sometimes reproached himself was a temptation that in fact he always overcame. He wrote much more than many authors who plume themselves on industry, and he wrote nothing with which he did not take pains.

What delighted him more than art or ideas or landscape was human nature, the oddity, the inconsistency, the surprisingness, of individual men and women and children. Goodness knows,

5

he loved words for their own sake. But he loved them first as clues to character. With what glee he would rub his hands as he revealed some incident or phrase that betrayed the secret workings of the heart! It was always a warm, glowing curiosity: he could make himself at home with a dead writer as if he were a living friend, putting himself in his place, patting him affectionately, not coldly probing or dissecting.

It was indeed the same genius for sympathy that made him both the most penetrating of critics and the most endearing of friends. No one in London was more widely and more wholeheartedly liked. He was adored by persons who detested one another. Wonderfully at home alike with politicians and artists and sportsmen, the confidant of Catholics and atheists, consulted by Tories and Socialists, he was comprehensive—but not, as are some men and more women, protean: he remained everywhere the same Desmond MacCarthy—genial, indulgent, amused, and, above all things, wise. He could be formidable: just because his sympathies were so wide, any conduct that was beyond their pale was stamped as black indeed, or at least as unpardonably silly. An Asquithian Liberal, he worked chiefly for Socialist and Conservative journals, and seldom entered into specifically political issues. But he took public events very hard, and in the years before the war he would become passionate in his support of Mr Churchill against both Right and Left.

Neither the fashionable nor the literary world (and he frequented both) is conspicuous for charity of tongue; yet never did one hear a malicious word against Desmond MacCarthy. (I have known only one other man, Francis Birrell, who was at once so clever and so generally beloved.) All his friends always wanted to see him; and his charm forced them to forgive him whenever he failed to keep an engagement. This was frequent: indeed, it used to be rumoured that he would promise to come to luncheon on the same day in Mayfair, Bloomsbury and Chelsea, so that wherever he found himself at 1.30 there would be a place laid for him. This story, besides being a fabrication, suggests a character the reverse of his. So far from looking ahead, he lived in the moment to an exceptional extent. His work was always done at the eleventh hour, with editors and printers tearing their hair. But this never prevented him for an instant from clarifying and enriching and titivating his prose. Nobody could exemplify better the rule that what is easy to read is hard to write.

Though he was by nature lenient, his concern for the craft of criticism made him admirably exacting both to others and to himself. As literary editor of *The New Statesman and Nation* he was tireless in training apprentices, like myself, first to prepare our reviews by use of the London Library, then to write and rewrite with tender care in the choice of epithet and adverb, idiom and cadence. As a coach he showed a patient rigour that would have astonished those of his friends who were never his pupils.

His fecklessness, which he took more tragically than his friends did, came presumably from his Irish forbears. His mother was half-French, half-German; and he enjoyed the curious mixture of his blood, from which he may have derived his exceptional breadth of sympathy. To England he owed his education at Eton and Trinity, Cambridge—both of which he loved profoundly—and his marriage to Mary Warre-Cornish, whose wit and delicacy, so dear to her friends, have been revealed to the public only in her too few books.

In which sort of writing did his talent gleam most beguilingly? He, I fancy, would have said in dramatic criticism. He doted on the theatre, and would analyse most solicitously mediocre plays that he could not have read through if they had been books. But he was a profound critic when he came to the Elizabethans, Ibsen, Chekhov or Shaw; and producers found his suggestions notably constructive. A volume called *Experience* reveals a gift for description that would have made him a virtuoso reporter. The same power is shewn in the volume I like perhaps the best, in which he paints the great writers and statesmen he had known. Then, again, the imagination with which he drew imaginary portraits of Voltaire and the Emperor

Francis Joseph suggests that he had it in him to be a fine biographer. It was characteristic of his criticism that he treated art almost always as an expression of personality.

When he left *The New Statesman and Nation* to succeed Sir Edmund Gosse as the leading critic on *The Sunday Times*, he found himself facing a far larger public. There was no need to modify his critical methods: he had always addressed himself to the cultivated general reader rather than to the specialist in 'Eng. Lit.' This earned him the contempt of those pedants who fancy that literature exists not to be enjoyed but to be evaluated. He was unruffled by rebukes that might have been applied with equal justice to all the critics he most admired, from Dryden and Johnson, through Coleridge, Sainte-Beuve and Pater, to Anatole France (now so unfashionable), Virginia Woolf and Sir Max Beerbohm.

Permanently influenced by Mr George Moore (the author of *Principia Ethica*), and a member of the old Bloomsbury circle, together with Leonard and Virginia Woolf, Clive and Vanessa Bell, Roger Fry, Lytton Strachey, E. M. Forster and Maynard Keynes, he was intellectually and aesthetically less austere than most of these, while sharing their impatience with humbug. A delighted interest in the variety of human experience was stronger in him than fastidiousness about the forms in which this was expressed. For the same reason, proud as he was to proclaim himself a highbrow, he made himself loved, as critic and broadcaster, by many who fancy that they hate highbrows. Though he wrote with an air of authority, he never gave himself airs, and his gusto was infectious. No other man I have known possessed such a genius for friendship; and for everyone who knew him the world since his death has become a colder place.

A PORTRAIT

by CYRIL CONNOLLY

His appearance is not as well known as it should be, for I do not think he often let himself be painted or photographed. There was something bird-like about him and the pen-name of 'Affable Hawk', under which he chose to succeed Sir John Squire's 'Solomon Eagle', fitted him exactly. He had a rather beak-like nose and the look of an alert but sedentary bird of prey. His voice must be very well known through the B.B.C. It was both manly and seductive and contained the essence of his charm; warm, friendly, independent and judicious, full of subtleties; the tenor of humanism. It spoke to everyone as if they were all his life-long fellow-guests at some delicious party and seemed to introduce himself to them by a touch of modest urbanity, as if to say, 'I do believe we are going to enjoy ourselves'. If one were to analyse his charm further, I think we would find that it was based on a desire to establish sympathy through imagery, usually taken from the world of smell, taste, touch and see, before proceeding to an intellectual judgment which might otherwise seem pretentious or alarming. Many of his talks and articles begin with some kind of pleasing social generalisation or an analogy that sets up a happy herd reaction, thus creating the intimacy in which his intellect loved to operate. This is sometimes dismissed as the 'desire to please' by those in whom neither the means nor the end are conspicuous. Where his convictions were involved, he never hesitated to displease, as long as he could do so without hurting people's feelings. Unlike many intellectuals, he understood that the feelings of stupid people are as vulnerable as those of the intelligent which led him to qualify many of his statements. In private he revealed a strong and wary mind and considerable impatience with all kinds of nonsense and

9

sentimentality. He was much more like his portrait of Roger
Fry than that of Robert Lynd. He was an elegiac natural
philosopher who all his life related small things to the perpetual
puzzle of man's nature and destiny or to the pattern of his virtues
and vices. Like Congreve, whom he much resembled both in
his taste and relish for words and by the love the great bore him,
he merited Gay's adjective 'unreproachful'. I doubt if a single
person could be found who might consider they had been
harshly treated by him. His laziness, however, like his un-
punctuality, was proverbial. He would often say to me that he
detested work in any form and I know he meant it. Of course,
like many idle people, he was forced by the roundabout methods
induced by his laziness into greater exertion than if he had
been the efficient servant of his will, and so his output in words
was in the end far larger than that of most writers with a reputation for assiduous productivity. The last moment—and especially the one after the last—appealed to all the gambler in him.

Sloth is the mark, in many artists, of a conflict between
genius and talent, the broken surface water where two deep
opposing currents battle. In his case, the element of genius
could not be segregated, as in his youth he hoped it would be,
into a novel, a play or a poem. It could do no more than
irradiate the talent which went into his criticism and his conversation, rendering him in those fields without a superior, but
ever conscious that he had not been able to give his friends the
supreme best of which he knew he was capable. Like Sainte-
Beuve, he strove to reconcile the wild romantic in him with the
studious epicurean and eventually allowed the one to forgive
the other. He never permitted his own self-disappointment to
influence adversely his judgments of other people. He was, in
every sense, the most generous of men. When he helped young
writers, he really did help them, he found them work, lent them
money and studied the particular originality through which
each could best distinguish himself. Here are some glimpses
of the process at work, taken from a diary kept when I was
twenty-three or twenty-four and Desmond, I suppose, about

thirty years older. I had already helped him with some arrears of journalism and been handsomely overpaid by three crisp fivers and two delicious late suppers at Kettners when the day's spell was finished and I had just been given by him my first assignment in print, on the *New Statesman*.

July 1927: 19th—Since Tripoli I have only been happy three times, working with Desmond, staying with Molly, and having Freddie to stay with me. Desmond's was the true happiness of liking one's work. Of course one has no business to expect to be happy. As he says 'Human life is almost unendurable'.

27th—Round to *New Statesman* to see Desmond who looks rather peaked and thin; dine on a mixed grill at Holborn Restaurant. He said Holmes and Watson often dined there. He tells me of his life at 23, said he was as idle as I was and it made him eventually ill. D. is impatient as well as intolerant and he thinks he knows all about me which is sometimes nettling. He will insist that I am not a highbrow. But I enjoy the Desert Island equality he always produces and was pleased when he gave me Maurice Baring's book to review. D. on his 'Life of Dr Watson'!

28th—Waking in Mecklenburgh Street. Feel rather haggard but my eye much better. Talk to Desmond while dressing. 'O dear, O dear,' he cried as he lay in bed. He seems to be getting involved in worries again. Short discussion on happiness. Desmond spoke of life as like his bayonet-instructor's advice: 'One downward twist, a turn of the wrist and the wound is incurable.'

. . . .

Marriage was discussed and I said that I was thrilled by the idea of it and appalled by the reality. Desmond said the reality was better than the idea, the great thing was to marry someone who was attractive even when tempers were roused, you must expect to be told unforgivable things, it was not wise to marry early. 'Men and women were really alike though it was fatal to treat them as if they were.'

At dinner he said the eighteenth century talked much slower than we did and were not afraid of eloquence and acting. Swinburne was the last person like this (imitating him). The Elizabethans were quite Latin. They talked even more slowly and were intolerably affected, wore gorgeous clothes, kissed each other in public, had no idea of privacy, swaggered and posed and read their sonnets to whoever sat next them. This was an amateurish age, it had swept away conventions and made no new ones, had removed all the

landmarks by which intimacy grew, psycho-analysis rubbed the last
moss off everyone. He said that everything you think is known.
Molly said a Lutheran Reformation was a great mistake. Desmond
said 'That might be, but without the Church of England there would
be no room for vaguely religious people, there would only be
Catholics and agnostics, sensitive Catholics and philistine atheists
as in Latin countries. Our church permitted people to love across
the barrier. But it was a pity Erasmus had not run the Reformation.
'All the same,' said Molly, 'if Desmond's ancestors had not been
religious, he would not have been the man he was.'

Desmond told a story of Swinburne taking off his shoes and
stockings on Wimbledon Common to wade into a pond to rescue a
wasp. He came out with it on the end of his stick and said 'It's only
a damned industrious bee.'

When one tries to penetrate more deeply into his character
the general impression he made becomes less definable. He liked
to say painful truths in a cheerful voice; however melancholy or
disillusioned seemed his mood, a hidden vitality helped to phrase
it. Even when ill he never left an impression of weariness
or emptiness. He put up with much incomprehension and
abuse from an editor for whom he had worked in the past and
who was killing himself with drink and he wrote nobly about him
when he perished, even as he had helped him when he was dying.
It is easy to be kind to the young, he was profoundly kind to
everybody. For that reason he had to avoid people, had to be
'unreliable', for so many plucked at his sleeve that he would
have had no clothes left. He was a wonderful travelling companion, he would read, sightsee, talk or play chess, conduct
imaginary conversations or invent imaginary animals, and
yet he remained a man of his century. One could never draw
closer to him than the kind of generalised Johnsonian intimacy
which he encouraged, and his look of warm pleasure or philosophic detachment could change to a strangely bleak and for-
bidding expression when, for instance, he was reading something which he thought 'bosh'. I suppose, as a man, he was
as ideal a companion as the breed has produced. Yet how stern
he grew (he even wrote me a letter about it), for 'a particular

note of reverence which crept into your voice when you spoke of Baudelaire'—to him Baudelaire was a poet with a lot of childish Satanism who had written a great many bad lines (he sent me some)—yet he looked rather like Baudelaire and, like him, was possessed by the demon of a dual standard who made all his activities seem unworthy. Some writers weighed very heavily on him—Byron, Coleridge for instance. As a young man he wished both to live fully and write fluently like Byron. His ancestors were men of action (one was a Regency rake) and he was very happy when acting as a special correspondent or getting more movement into his life than the critic's arm-chair warranted. But we live in an age when we cannot both be Byron and write like him. Genius can only be extracted from talent when it is subjected to a pressure that the possessor will do everything to avoid. Desmond accepted the way of Montaigne, rather than the way of Pascal; of Diderot rather than of Rousseau, and so became the man as well as the writer he was; wise, just, deep, generous, acute and fearless. Among all his felicitious imagery, one expression is beginning to stick. It is 'bird-happy'.

I suppose I knew about half a dozen 'Desmonds' and all of them had their share of his six and seventy years of life. There was Desmond in his relationship to Bloomsbury, which was rather peculiar. They had difficulty in forgiving his catholicity of taste; it seemed incomprehensible to them that he could like so many of the same things, and share the same Cambridge east wind of intellectual integrity and radicalism while finding so much sympathy for their opposites. This led them, perhaps, to under-rate him, as in Virginia Woolf's portrait of Bernard in *The Years*. He distrusted their pride of intellect—by that sin fell the 'apostles'—and they were alarmed, I believe, by his robust commonsense and social graces. Then there was his relationship with his cronies like Maurice Baring—immensely gay, simple, childish, one of those luxury friendships possible only in a world of leisure. Besides an interest in love and literature they laughed together a great deal, though Maurice did most of the laughing. It was a deep, formal, fashionable relationship that seemed to go on for ever. With Logan Pearsall-Smith the picture changed: affectionate, teasing, curious, free-minded yet always slightly shocked, Logan was like an American collector who had acquired a piece of great price which he was always afraid of losing and yet sometimes thought might be a fake. He forgave him everything (he had very little to forgive) except his admiration for Belloc—and with Belloc and Chesterton there were relationships too, as with Robert Trevelyan and so many more. Their games of chess were a delight to watch. Though ten years older than Desmond, Logan would get over-excited and squeal for mercy like an ensnared rabbit. Desmond always relented. 'Let me see, let me see'—Logan would puff—'my Queen's attacked—she can't go there—she can't go there—but she can go *there*', and he would hop her over an intervening pawn. 'No, Logan, I'm afraid she can't go there'—'And she can't go there—why, she's lost. Desmond, Desmond let me take that back'—'then you'd better take back the move before'—'I wasn't concentrating. I can't get over what you told me about the C . . . . s. Now let me see, my Queen's attacked. But supposing I attack your Queen? —let's see if Lady Desborough and Lady Salisbury and all your grand friends can help you now. Ha! How's this?—Check!' 'Then I go here and you still lose your Queen.' 'Hoo, hoo— Desmond let me take that back!'

Then there was all his worldly life; the fifty years of great houses, grand dinners and large intimate luncheons where Henry James, George Moore, Arthur Balfour, Augustine Birrell shone like red suns and talked and ate and passed into the silence and then his close relationship with the whole family of Asquiths. In this world, the 'grand monde', he was exquisitely courteous, he had the perfect manners of another age. His voice was silvery, modulated, his tact extreme, for it was more than tact. He knew not only how everybody pictured themselves, how they expected to be treated, but he saw right through to the inner aspirations of their personality, as if he had known them as children. He enjoyed for a while the comfortable, the glamorous, the great, but he was not a snob; it was they who needed him and, after his solo, he would soon pack up the wonderful flute of his conversation and slide away to his office to enjoy the one aristocracy which this aristocrat admitted, the writers who, from Horace onwards, had enriched his imagination and stimulated his judgment, even as he quickens ours.

ACKNOWLEDGMENTS

THE essays in *Memories* were selected and prepared for publication in book form by Mr Robert Kee.

The publishers' grateful acknowledgments are due to the following for permission to reprint material used in this book: *The Sunday Times* for very many of the essays which first appeared in their columns; *Life and Letters* for 'Bennett, Wells and Trollope'; *Nash's Pall Mall Magazine* for 'William Somerset Maugham'; the Syndics of the Cambridge University Press for 'Leslie Stephen' (the 1937 Leslie Stephen lecture which has been abridged); Messrs George Newnes for 'Max Beerbohm' (first published in *The Strand*); Sir Maurice Bowra and MacMillan and Co. Ltd., for the quotation from his translation of Lermontov; Messrs Jonathan Cape Ltd. and Messrs Chatto Windus Ltd. respectively for the quotations from W. H. Davies and Lytton Strachey.

And to the following for their help: Mr Raymond Mortimer, Mr Cyril Connolly for advice; Mr J. W. Lambert for advice and for reading the proofs—a service he rendered Sir Desmond MacCarthy in his lifetime; and finally to Lady MacCarthy for her advice and patience over the choice of these essays.

Contents

WRITERS

BENNETT, WELLS AND TROLLOPE

1930

THE last words of the third volume of Arnold Bennett's Diaries are: 'Monday, December 31st 1929. This year I have written 304,000 words: 1 play, 2 films, 1 small book on religion, and about 80 or 81 articles. Also I lost a full month in rehearsals, and a full month, no, six weeks, on holidays.'

These Diaries are likely to have much the same effect on Arnold Bennett's reputation as Trollope's *Autobiography* had on his: at first they will damage, but, in the end, enhance it. Arnold Bennett may be more or less ignored for many years, as Trollope was ignored, but his work, too, will revive. He stands in a similar relation to his own age, and his best qualities are the same—straightforwardness and keen interest in all that occupied the attention of ordinary men in his day. Those times are not so pleasant for us to contemplate as Trollope's, but that is partly the result of our propinquity.

How completely Trollope had dropped out of recognition by the end of the nineteenth century was once brought home to me by his widow. She was, when I made her acquaintance, well over eighty, and a very vigorous old woman with downright opinions, a tart tongue, and an energetic countenance. She was then living with her niece, Miss Bland, next door but one to my home in Cheyne Gardens. On Empire Day the balcony of their house was a-flutter with flags, and if May 24th happened to be fine, the small oblong garden at the back was carpeted with Union Jacks. My attention was first drawn to the old lady who on sunny days used to sit there, crocheting, by an occasional sound of such extraordinary violence that, until its origin had been ascertained, it drew the heads of her neighbours to their back windows. It resembled the noise of someone falling from a height into a cucumber frame: Mrs Anthony Trollope had sneezed. She must have been something of a tyrant, for on one occasion Miss Bland came round for help in an emergency—their two servants, terrified of giving notice to their mistress, had suddenly and silently decamped. This, I think, was the beginning of our closer acquaintance. I used to call sometimes and gaze at her with pleasure and curiosity, fancying I could see in her traces of Trollope's spirited straightforward heroines, whom I loved also for their resemblance to some of my own country cousins. I had read the best-known Trollopes with admiration, but I had found it difficult to procure his out-of-the-way novels. One afternoon I ventured to ask her to lend me *The Vicar of Bullhampton*, and—here is the incident which brought home to me how completely Trollope had dropped out of recognition—I had difficulty in making her believe that I wanted to read it. Too many years have passed to allow of my reporting the conversation which followed, but I know it began with her looking at me hard and by an equally searching question: 'Are you sure you are not asking for it to please *me*?' and that when I protested that I had the greatest admiration for her husband's work, she said: 'Well, I'm very glad to hear it, but I thought young people of your age despised my husband's books.' She let me, however, take *The Vicar* away, and after that *The Claverings*, *Ralph the Heir*, and others.

There is always a slump in the reputation of a novelist after his death, and this is likely to be deep if he has been prolific. Bennett astonished us, as Trollope astonished his contemporaries, by the amount he wrote. As soon as one book was finished he began another. Sometimes he had two or three books on the stocks at the same time. He also left behind him his Journals, which contain in the original over a million words. All this shows how delightful, and even necessary to him, the occupation of writing was; writing was his relief, his joy, and a condition of self-satisfaction, as well as his profession. There are many interesting entries in his Journals. Though it is likely that most readers will find them dry, it is their dryness and bleakness that I like. They are the Journals of a man who passes a drag-net through the river of life which has flowed past him during the day, in the hope of catching a few little fish. They may or may not be worth eating afterwards, but he can't be sure. Anyhow, he thinks, the mere habit of recording experience increases the chance of not having lived in vain. We hate to think that so much that happens to us passes away completely, and A. B.'s sense of purposeful economical living, which showed in his dread of wasting time, his passionate punctuality, his pedantic orderliness, accounts also for his having kept this long, steady diary for thirty-five years. He could not bear to waste even valueless scraps of experience. The chief value of his diary to us is that it helps us towards a better understanding of his art and his relation to it.

Arnold Bennett's greatest qualities are those which are wronged by excessive praise. He was an exceedingly honest, unpretentiously objective novelist. He was astonishingly productive, and, though he spared no pains with each book in turn, they were of most uneven merit. How cold that commendation sounds! Yet it was thus men wrote of Trollope when he died in '83. They said that he was a most honest, capable author; they said he deserved his big income for having entertained them well; they said that possibly readers in days to come might value his work as documents depicting contemporary English life, but they doubted if his work was a contribution to English literature. Trollope appeared to the discriminating as an honest journeyman of letters. Did he not write every day with clockwork regularity, and begin a new novel on the day he finished the last? How unlike an artist! Was he not always interested in his market? How unlike an artist! His prose was sound and pedestrian, and that was all you could say for it. How unlike an artist! They would never have dreamt of ranking him with George Eliot, whose work was so full of interesting philosophical reflections, or with Thackeray, who wrote so much better.

Well, fifty years have passed since Trollope died, eighty since he began to write, and he stands high and permanently among English novelists. When we want to know how people lived and thought in mid-Victorian days, we undoubtedly do turn to Trollope, but it is not for that reason he is most often read. That does not account for the modern library and pocket editions of his novels which today follow each other at intervals. We read Trollope because he is a trustworthy creator of normal men and women, because he enters so sympathetically into their lives, their joys, failings, difficulties, and because he makes their surroundings vivid to us, their relations to those above and below them in the social scale. This is what Arnold Bennett did for contemporary life. His merit is his abounding interest in the actual and his power of conveying that interest to us. But Trollope had the advantage of inheriting a stable set of values with a solid body of contemporary opinion behind them. He could appeal to standards which were universally accepted. It made his picture of life more superficial, but more firm in outline. Bennett was born into a restless, investigating age: an age which was digging at the roots of motives. He was forced to go deeper into human nature, and thus in his finest work, *The Old Wives' Tale*, *Clayhanger* and its sequels, and in many chapters scattered up and down his novels, we also apprehend human beings, not merely in relation to the social system or current morality, but in relation to the forces beneath the surface which control human life. This requires a more penetrating kind of imagination. His common sense was not as firm as Trollope's; he was more sensitive, but he carried even into the more obscure recesses of human experience the same lantern of downright honesty, the same kind of sympathy. He, too, was one of the least egotistic of writers.

Compare him one moment in this respect with a novelist whose name, with his, is often mentioned in the same breath —Wells. Bennett and Wells, Wells and Bennett—we think of them as two great twin-brethren, who by means of stories illuminated our times. Wells did so largely by means of interpolated discourse: he always had a lecturer's wand in his hand while he narrated—but that is not the main difference between them. They both show the changes which are going on before our eyes, but one feels when one reads Wells' books that his perceptions have always been sharpened by the way in which the confusion of the existing order has impinged upon *himself*, has baffled, tortured, and amused *him*. His fiction is auto-biography in disguise, doctored and altered often beyond recognition, but in spirit, at any rate, autobiography; just as his abstract thinking has the air of always having been prompted by the exigencies of his own predicament at a particular moment, however disinterestedly it may have been pursued. Thanks to being such a bundle of conflicting sensibilities, reactions and passions—so 'human', in fact, to use a tag—this reflection of a personal response to life was extraordinarily rich in results. Wells showed us things worth seeing because he was so *personal*; but Bennett showed them so well because he forgot himself.

Compared with Wells, Bennett was an 'eye' without a character behind it. But what was, however, behind that eye was a sympathy which enabled him to find ordinary characters as interesting as they are to themselves. Wells's characters, when they are not projections of himself, are as interesting as they are to *him*; that is to say, interesting in a very different way. Bennett's method is what we call the objective method. Now it is easier to see the greatness of an author in work which obviously depends upon the author himself for its charm, excitement and power. Such work drives us at once to think of the author's ardour and penetration. In Bennett's finest work we forgot him, and it was only on second thoughts that we saw that to present character and events so impartially required rare qualities, intellectual disinterestedness and self-less sympathy. Anyone can see how much of an artist a writer is if his attitude towards his own work is of a self-delighting kind. Bennett was much more of an artist than many people were inclined to believe. The fact was obscured by his standing off from what he described, and also by his power of putting through any job he set his hand to, so that he finished many a book which made no call on his highest faculties. I have used the metaphor I am about to use before, but it explains best what I mean.

You know those little electric motors which can be fixed to sailing boats and drive them along when the wind drops? They have spoilt sailing, though they are exceedingly convenient. Arnold Bennett was an artist who was born (unfortunately for us, yes, and for him too) with such an attachment. He could move rapidly in any direction he wished without waiting for the breath of inspiration; he could make progress without tacking. He was cursed with an irrelevant and impartial efficiency. He could write a readable article on anything from Proust to the 'three-piece' dress; he could make 'a job' of any theme though he had only a craftsman's interest in it; and the result was that he was unable to distinguish easily between what he could do, and what he could do best. He constantly confused in himself the conscientiousness of the craftsman with that of the artist.

The pivot round which the world of Trollope revolves is the country house. His England is England when the landed-gentry were still uppermost in the realm, when power meant property accompanied by definite responsibilities, privileges and standards. He often shifted the focus of his tales to the professions—to the Law, Parliament, the Church—but the great pervading fact of the social scene, as he painted it, was the nobleman with his thousands of acres in his castle, or the squire who was a little king in his own corner of the county. Trollope was amused by the relations of small men to big men and of great to greater, and intensely interested in the pride with which they severally recognised their obligations to each other and to themselves. Like his own characters, he accepted the hierarchy; and he watched with buoyant sympathy the vicissitudes of his heroes and heroines who were—the phrase is most characteristic of him—'growing towards the light'. He revelled in their success, partly because it *was* success—for he accepted the social hierarchy with a robust matter-of-factness entirely free from either mean envy or uneasy admiration—but chiefly because the process of getting on was itself a thorough test of character. At every turn he was able to compare those who were ready to sacrifice their proper pride, their spiritual decency or their sincerity of heart in order to 'get on' with those who refused to compromise their 'manliness' (to use a favourite Victorian word), or their 'womanliness', which meant putting the claims of the heart before everything but duty. In all this Trollope was the chronicler of his times, and that he was such a chronicler adds to the importance of his work.

When I survey the work of Arnold Bennett, passing his stories in rapid review, I am struck by his resemblance to Trollope in this respect. It is a different England he paints, and to me not nearly such an attractive one, but I see reasons for thinking that his picture of society will interest posterity historically in the same way. The pivot is no longer the Hall and landed property, but the Luxury Hotel and inexhaustible dividends—the power of huge floating fortunes, and the fascination of irresponsible, exaggerated spending. I am not at all sure that these features of our civilisation, which caught the eye of Bennett, will not prove to be the very ones which will stand out for posterity looking back on it. Bennett accepted the hierarchy of Capitalism (with some reservations) in the same uncritical robust way that Trollope accepted the social order of his day; and his stories, also, described men and women 'growing towards the light'. His constant theme is the comedy and gratification of getting into the golden sunlight before you have really any right to, and then of establishing yourself firmly there. He was never tired of describing the joy of newly-acquired possessions, and the triumph of the parvenu at successfully pretending he is not impressed by what really thrills him. His novels, too, are largely about 'getting on', not, in the sense Trollope's are, about reaching the social shelf which your abilities, character, and education entitle you to, but about getting richer in a fluid, chaotic society—being able to afford the finest suite in a grand hotel, the most costly flat, the best yacht, the most impeccably dressed daughters, and making magnificent gestures with a cheque book. Many people thought this was due to vulgarity in Bennett; the vulgarity was in the age he depicted. 'Getting on' in the modern world is often a matter of bounce and luck—you may get rich overnight; success in Bennett's novel was therefore not such a fine test of character as it was in Trollope's days. This was a loss to Bennett the novelist. But in his early *Five Towns* stories he showed clearly the grit which went to making a start in life, and he created that commercial and competitive atmosphere in which it was plausible that citizens should regard the making of money as the test of manhood. In his middle period, in *The Card* and its sequels, he described amusingly that plucky and innocent impudence which often leads by short cuts to fortune. His strength was to reflect, like Trollope, the standards of his times, and it was not his fault that the average hero was in his day the parvenu, and no longer the man who knew his right place. Trollope saw clearly the irresponsible selfishness of the pompous old Duke of Omnium, and the hollow pretentiousness of the De Courcys, but he would not deny that it was a fine thing to be a duke. Bennett refused to deny that it was a fine thing to be a millionaire, though he was capable of making fun of millionaire bluster and weakness.

He was under the impression that his descriptions of wealthy life were full of glaring and biting social satire. We once had a brief correspondence about this point. I had written, when reviewing *Lilian*, 'I have a feeling, now and then, while reading Mr Bennett, that he does not *want* to blow the gaff; as if he had made up his mind that it was silly, if not dishonest, to be disillusioned about making lots of money and having "good times", there being so little else in life. It would explain why he usually chooses to see these things through a pair of eyes which the reader can believe were easily beglamoured, those of some enterprising young business man, or woman, suddenly lifted out of financial embarrassment. My quarrel with him is that he does not let *us* see round that view of them. . . .

'He is a thorough artist as a craftsman . . . but his response to life is singularly uncoloured by aesthetic emotions. Their place is taken by gusto for prestige values. What would happen if Mr Bennett ceased to think it a crowning moment in life to drive a twenty-foot motor up to a hotel, where the air can only be breathed at the cost of a shilling a minute, and to order a dinner of which every course was out of season? There is always some satire in his picture of plutocratic privileges, but satire is lost in sympathy. Would not the romance of the Five Towns suffer too, if the candle for which the game was played was not brightly lit? Or, rather, would not that romance become once more tragic in quality, as it did in *The Old Wives' Tale*?'

Now Bennett was utterly without resentment when you criticised him as long as he believed that you were not trying to be clever at his expense, but stating a genuine opinion. I have never met a writer more magnanimous in that respect. I was constantly writing about his novels and plays in a way which would have made most authors drop my acquaintance. All he did in this instance was to write me a letter emphasising that his novel was crammed with social satire, and that I was blind to the beauty and romance of modern life—it was *I* who was unaesthetic. (There was truth in this charge.) But when *Mr Prohack* appeared, I found myself again in doubt whether the book was intended as a picture of futility or attainment. Was the sudden good fortune of the Prohack family after all a Timon's feast, a matter of warm water under silver dish-covers? It looked rather like it. Yet a doubt remained. With his intellect Bennett constantly assented to the proposition that the solid happiness of possessing £20,000 a year and a son who is a financial magnate could be easily exaggerated; yet his temperament kept shouting enthusiastically as he told the story of the Prohacks, in a tone very far from that of Timon's angry irony, 'Uncover, dogs, and lap!' The voice of his temperament was louder than that of his intellect. Hence the reader's confused impression at the close of books about the rich, which nevertheless did contain much social satire, and satire particularly directed against the getting and spending of money. That particular story closed with a description of a magnificent yacht on which young Prohack never sails but takes tea at intervals, and (almost in the spirit of *Bouvard and Pécuchet*) with Mr Prohack taking up routine work to again make more money which he does not want.

Although his material is, in the ordinary sense of the word, unromantic, his interpretation of life is thoroughly romantic. The essence of all romanticism is to make an individual's feeling about things the sole test of their value. The state of feeling called 'passion' is essentially romantic, for everybody knows that the immense value it attributes to a particular person has no objective truth. All Bennett's characters are passionate, whether it is about another human being or a printing-press, or anything else, and their passion throws a glamour over the sordidness and squalor of the Five Towns. We feel, as we read, serious doubts whether the Five Towns are not in some incomprehensible way superior to Athens or Florence! We lose all sense of an external standard. Bennett's finest book is also a romantic one, but it deals with *the tragedy of romanticism*. In *The Old Wives' Tale* he rose above the point of view of the characters themselves, whose impulses and desires glorified disproportionately one thing after another. We were made to feel that the alchemy of the will cannot gild the ravages of time. Time not only takes away attractiveness from the body and activity from the mind, but also that internal generating power which makes ordinary things seem worth while. How sleepy and dull the two sisters are at the end of the book! He was at his greatest when he brought his characters up against the fact of death and the injuries of old age. It was that that made *The Old Wives' Tale* so fine a book, and his pathos in many an episode so grim, large, merciful and impressive.

LYTTON STRACHEY

AND THE ART OF BIOGRAPHY

circa 1934

WE are all readers of biographies nowadays. Indeed, biography has become a popular rival to fiction. It will be said that one characteristic of twentieth century literature was that its fiction tended to become more like biography and its biography more like fiction. Today in the novel the story often goes by the board. We are given instead a life of a man from cradle to the grave, or at any rate, a series of scenes from that long journey; while biographers use the novelist's privilege of imagining what their heroes or heroines were thinking and feeling at any particular moment, though documentary evidence for that is scanty or non-existent. I remember feeling some impatience with Herr Ludwig when in his *Life of Napoleon* he took upon himself to state not only that Napoleon's stern grey eyes filled with tears as he gazed from a window of the Tuileries at the mob below, but actually what thoughts were passing behind those eyes.

This method of writing a man's life as though he were the hero in a novel is the easiest way of making biography attractive. It results in readable books, but not in biographies which the reader can respect as well as enjoy.

In the nineteenth century, the biographer was sometimes driven through lack of material to writing with an extreme tentativeness, and tiresome the results were. A parody of history written in the subjunctive mood will illustrate what I mean. The biographer had set himself the task of writing an account of an English Abbess in the tenth century, one Osmunda Regalis. The poor man was trying, as you will see, to make bricks without straw.

Amid the ancient cloisters of which a few crumbling ruins now mark—in the opinion of one uncertain archaeological authority—the ruins of what was doubtless long known (if it was known at all) as St. Osmund's nunnery, surrounded by a bevy of maidens, among whom the daughters of a Hengist *may well* have been found side by side with the ancestors of a Plantagenet, we can picture her at her work—we can glow with enthusiasm at the picture of the noble spinster, who, it may be, embodied in her striking character all the vigour infused by the Roman invader into the sluggish Anglo-Saxon stock (for the latinisation of her name would appear to indicate a mixed parentage), directing the spiritual and material affairs of an abbey, which was *perhaps*—as why should it not have been?—a more popular centre of culture and refinement than any inferior institution of the same kind.

In short: Gibbon without labour.

Now today no one is going to read such havering tentative stuff—and quite right too. But at least it is *honest*. Today the biographer of that dim Abbess would boldly project as ascertained truth a picture of Osmunda Regalis among her nuns, composed out of details he had managed to pick up from his general reading about the period. Would that be an improvement? Well, certainly—from the point of view of readableness. But the price is a loss of integrity.

A biographer is an artist who is on oath, and anyone who knows anything about artists, knows that that is almost a contradiction in terms. That is why first-rate biography is rarer than first-rate fiction. Biography is undoubtedly an art. But if it is an art, how are we to define it? I think the simplest way is to say that a biography must aim at being a truthful record of an individual life, composed as a work of art. If one stops to consider the implications of that, one realises that biography must be more difficult than the art of fiction, for the biographer cannot invent those circumstances which might illustrate best the character he is depicting. He has to take those incidents as he finds them. All he can do is to arrange facts as effectively as possible. He must neither alter nor ignore them, however much that might help him to bring out even an essential truth about his subject. And yet he must impose some pattern on the disorder of life, or his book will only be a quarry from which some other man may be able some day to construct a building.

During the First World War, in May 1918, to be precise, a volume of short biographies appeared which had an extraordinary influence on the writing of biography not only in this country, but abroad, in France, in Germany and America. One of those short lives began as follows:

During the year 1883, a solitary English gentleman was to be seen, wandering, with a thick book under his arm, in the neighbourhood of Jerusalem. His unassuming figure, short and slight, with its half-gliding, half-tripping motion, gave him a boyish aspect, which contrasted oddly, but not unpleasantly, with the touch of grey on his hair and whiskers. There was the same contrast—enigmatic and attractive—between the sunburnt-brick-red complexion—the hue of the seasoned traveller—and the large blue eyes with their look of almost childish sincerity. To the friendly enquirer, he would explain, in a low, soft and very distinct voice, that he was engaged in elucidating four questions—the site of the Crucifixion, the line of division between the tribes of Benjamin and Judah, the identification of Gibeon, and the position of the Garden of Eden. He was also, he would add, most anxious to discover the spot where the Ark first touched ground, after the subsidence of the Flood: he believed, indeed, that he had solved *that* problem, as a reference to some passages in the book which he was carrying would show.

This singular person was General Gordon, and his book was the Holy Bible.

Now how like the opening of a novel that is! It even recalls that once popular figure with which so many romances have begun—'The Solitary Horseman'. Shades of Walter Scott, Marryat and G. P. R. James!

But examine this opening passage for a moment from another point of view: there is not a detail in this picture for which the biographer could not have given a reference: the half-gliding, half-tripping gait, the large blue eyes with that odd look of childish sincerity in them; the suggestion of something boyish in this grizzled, sunburnt English *gentleman*; and note, through the description of his peculiar interests, that it is at once sug-

B

gested that he is not like other men. He is a crank, maybe, or perhaps one who might be both crank and mystic; certainly a man unlikely to think or act on the same evidence as practical men. Thus, the note which is going to run through the whole story is struck vigorously at once. Sure enough, what we are about to follow is an account of the embarrassments, half comic, half tragic, which others encountered while attempting to work with such a man as General Gordon.

I do not propose to discuss here how near to truth Lytton Strachey's account of Gordon is. What I want to insist upon is that he handles his theme like an *artist*. He was dealing with a man so different, even in his religious conceptions, from his co-religionists, that it is said that the Sunday before he started for the Sudan he drove round to a number of churches to take Communion *as many times as possible*, and start thus brimfull of God. Strachey does not tell this anecdote (perhaps it is not well enough authenticated), nor another which also shows the curiously *primitive* nature of Gordon's mind. A diplomat, once attached to Lord Cromer in Egypt, has described an interview at which Gordon offered him, in oriental fashion, a present of some value. The embarrassed young official said, of course, that he could not possibly take presents, which seemed strangely to perturb the General. At last, having tried repeatedly to force him to change his mind, Gordon said: 'Well, won't you accept my penknife?' The idea at the back of his insistence must have been a kind of faith in magic: if only he could induce this official to accept something which had once belonged to him, he, Gordon, would have an influence over him. Well, it was a man capable of entertaining *such* ideas, yet in other respects so strong a master of events and men, with whom the biographer had to deal. In striking the note he did at the beginning, Lytton Strachey thus showed an instinctive grasp of the biographer's art.

That art is part of my subject. I do not want to delay upon the history of it. But to settle Lytton Strachey's place among biographers, it is necessary to call to mind a few facts about the history of biography. Early biography is uncritical. The impulse behind it is the spirit which inspired that famous chapter in Ecclesiasticus, 'Let us now praise famous men'. In this spirit, Plutarch wrote his *Lives*. Closely and naturally connected with this impulse is the *hortatory* motive, '—to hold up an example before others'. Thus in early biography the stress is upon great deeds or great virtues. The lives of men were first written to inspire wonder or imitation, and hero worship and hagiography have left their mark upon subsequent biography to this day. There still survives a vague feeling in many readers that there is something wrong when a biographer fails to describe his subject as greater and better than other men. If he was *not*, why write his life at all? Anyhow, the *emphasis* must be upon his virtues. There is probably no respect in which we differ more from our remoter ancestors than in the kind of interest we take in human nature. If we found ourselves back in the Middle Ages what we should miss quite as much as creature comforts would be gossip. Our earlier forebears were chiefly interested in human motives in relation to sin. In outward behaviour they were of course interested, and Chaucer certainly had the makings of a gossip. But the impression which that old world makes on us is—to use a word from the vocabulary of modern psychologists—a world of complete 'extroverts'. What a picture Chaucer might have drawn of John of Gaunt, if only it had entered his head, or anyone else's at the time, that such a thing was worth doing. Until you come to Cavendishe's *Life of Wolsey*, there is no biography in English which has a tincture of art. Cavendishe is full of vivid detail. He tells us how Wolsey sniffed at his aromatic orange when worried by suitors, how quickly he sometimes threw himself off his mule. Cavendishe is as vivid as any modern biographer could wish when he comes to Wolsey's arrest. Yet it is not the use of detail, not the use of anecdote, which distinguished Cavendishe's biography from those written before. After all, William of Malmesbury had peppered his chronicles with anecdotes, saying, and with how much truth, that stories cannot displease any reader unless he is as proud and morose as Cato. No: what distinguished Cavendishe's *Life of Wolsey* was that it was the first not written in *honour* of a hero, but round a thesis—an idea, in this case, *sic transit gloria mundi*, that theme which Shakespeare caught in the famous speech:

> Farewell! a long farewell to all my greatness.
> This is the state of man.

This conception of Wolsey's life, this thesis, imposed a unity on the story and a disinterestedness towards the subject of it which was not to reappear again in biography for almost a hundred years. Only when we come to Walton and his *Lives* does another artist in biography appear, and he is not so disinterested. Walton is charming, limpid, balanced, the most amiable of all English biographers. He is inspired by the most genuine love of goodness—at least of the placid goodness he understands so well—and he is the most modest of biographers. But the point I wish to stress is that Walton's beautiful reverence for goodness as he felt and understood it really links his *Lives* with hagiography. His theme is the goodness of the men he draws, not the men themselves. It is not until we reach the eighteenth century that the technique of modern biography begins to develop. It is Dr Johnson who not only supplies the first masterly portrait of a *man*, in his life of Richard Savage, but formulates the principles of biography as a distinct art. Johnson himself was incorrigibly preoccupied with human nature. He denied that a biographer's first business was to deal with those of a man's actions which had become part of history. He should, he said, 'pass slightly over those performances and incidents which produce vulgar greatness, to lead the thoughts into domestic privacies and to display the minute details of private life'. To show first and foremost what a man had been in himself, that was the biographer's task, while the *interest* of biography depended on its truth. 'Biography has often been allotted to writers', Johnson wrote, 'who seem very little acquainted with the nature of their task, or very negligent about the performance. They rarely afford any other account than might be collected from public papers, but imagine themselves writing a life when they exhibit a chronological series of actions or preferments; and so little regard the manners or behaviour of their heroes, that more knowledge may be gained of a man's real character by a short conversation with one of his servants, than from a formal and studied narrative begun with his pedigree, and ended with his funeral.'

'If we owe regard to the memory of the dead', he also wrote, 'there is yet more respect to be laid to knowledge, to virtue and truth. There are many who think it an act of piety to hide the faults or failings of their friends, even when they can no longer suffer by their detection. We therefore see whole ranks of characters adorned with uniform panegyric, and not to be known from one another but by extrinsic and casual circumstances.' Johnson's great biographer evidently took these precepts to heart. Of that most famous of English biographies I will say nothing except that the circumstances which made the writing of it possible are so seldom combined that Boswell can not often be a model to others. How well that phrase of Johnson's 'whole ranks of characters adorned with uniform panegyric and not to be known from one another but by extrinsic and casual circumstances' describes the run of nineteenth century biographies.

In the breakdown of reticence towards the end of the nineteenth century the influence of candid autobiography must be reckoned with; and before turning back to Lytton Strachey and to what was most individual in his handling of this art, we must mention a more immediate precursor in spirit, namely, Sir Edmund Gosse. Gosse's *Father and Son*, a remarkable cross between autobiography and biography, came in tone as well as in theme nearest to *Eminent Victorians*. Edmund Gosse had been able to record in the person of his father and in his own experience a tragi-comic clash between an age of belief and one of scepticism, a theme which constantly inspired Lytton Strachey's irony.

As practically nothing has been written about Lytton Strachey as a man, it may not be uninteresting if I attempt to give you some idea of him, for I knew him well.

He was born at Clapham in 1880; he was the last but two of a long family, and a family which for several generations had been remarkable for ability. When Francis Galton was making his researches into hereditary talent he examined, together with the Darwins and the Butlers, the Pollocks and other families who had distinguished themselves for several generations, the careers of the Stracheys.

Lytton Strachey was born, then, into what we may term the intellectual aristocracy of England, and he belonged to the administrative class. His grandfather, Edward Strachey, an Anglo-Indian of considerable importance in his day, was a friend of Carlyle. They made an excursion to Paris together in the pre-railroad days and—it is Carlyle who tells the story— at the end of the journey the postillion asked for a tip. Edward Strachey curtly refused, adding 'vous avez drivé devilish slow'.

I repeat this small anecdote for the sake of his grandson's comment upon it, which is characteristic of Lytton Strachey's attitude towards all forms of John Bullishness.

'The reckless insularity of this remark', he wrote, 'illustrates well enough the extraordinary change which had come over the English governing classes since the eighteenth century. Fifty years earlier a cultivated Englishman would have piqued himself upon answering the postilion in the idiom and the accent of Paris. But the Napoleonic Wars, the industrial revolution, the romantic revival, the Victorian spirit, had brought about a relapse from the suavity of the eighteenth century culture; the centrifugal forces always latent in English life had triumphed, and men's minds had shot off into the grooves of eccentricity and provincialism.'

He proceeds to notice the flux and reflux of these tendencies in the history of our literature: 'the divine amenity of Chaucer followed by the no less divine idiosyncrasy of the Elizabethans;

the *exquisite vigour* of the eighteenth century followed by the *rampant vigour* of the nineteenth'; and (please note these words) 'today, the return once more to the Latin elements in our culture, the revulsion from the Germanic influences which obsessed our grandfathers, the preference for what is swift, what is well-arranged, and what is not too *good*'. Too edifying, Strachey means.

I ask you to note those passages for two reasons, one connected with his own work (he himself was the chief representative of that revulsion and that preference), and the other connected with himself and his influence upon his own generation. He had been a delicate child, and after one term at a private school, he had been sent to Leamington College. This choice was probably made on grounds of health. (I know nothing of Leamington College beyond the fact that it was one of the minor public schools.) But this choice was of some importance —he thereby escaped the more powerful and possibly more agreeable influence of one of the *great* public schools. Lytton Strachey's individualism would probably have survived that. But as it was, what is called 'the public school spirit', 'team-work', 'playing the game' and so forth, remained notions, not only repulsive, but to a large extent incomprehensible, to him. He not only disliked and feared the public school spirit but thought it absurd and grotesque.

You cannot imagine a youth more utterly unsatisfactory from, say, Kipling's point of view, than the long, limp, pale young man with pince-nez and a small rather dismal moustache, who came up to Trinity, Cambridge, in 1899. He had left Leamington in 1897 for Liverpool University, where he attended Walter Raleigh's lectures and had read history in a desultory fashion; it was a letter from Walter Raleigh announcing that a distinctly remarkable undergraduate was about to join us, which largely determined Lytton Strachey's circle of friends at the university.

As he kept those friends all his life; as that London set of writers and artists, known afterwards as 'Bloomsbury', in which he was the most prominent figure, was really an off-shoot or colony of Cambridge at the beginning of the century (with Leslie Stephen's two daughters, Virginia Woolf and Vanessa Bell, added), I shall try to indicate the spirit of that Cambridge generation to which I also belonged.

We were not much interested in politics. Abstract speculation was much more absorbing. Philosophy was much more interesting to us than public causes. The wave of Fabian socialism, which affected some of Lytton Strachey's younger contemporaries like Rupert Brooke, had not reached Cambridge in my time. What we chiefly discussed were those 'goods' which were ends in themselves; and these ends, for which the rest of life was only a scaffolding, could be subsumed under three heads: the search for truth, aesthetic emotions and personal relations—love and friendship.

Those who have been to a university will remember how each decade, as far as the intellectual life of the young is concerned, tends to be dominated by some unusually gifted man. The dominating influence when Lytton Strachey came up was metaphysical, embodied in G. E. Moore and Bertrand Russell who had shaken confidence in the Idealism of McTaggart. Thus Amurath to Amurath succeeds. Lytton Strachey himself was the next influence. He remained at Cambridge after he had taken his degree, a second in History, sitting for a Fellowship at Trinity till 1905 and writing a dissertation on Warren Hastings. The curious can read that essay in his posthumous volume *Characters and Commentaries.* It is an elegant and surprisingly mature piece of work. No doubt he was attracted to the subject through the connection of his family with India, but it was not a subject particularly suited to his hand, and it failed to win him a Fellowship. Meanwhile, as I said, he had become a leader among the young, not only through his culture, his wit and the discrimination of his taste, but thanks above all to the vehement and passionate nature of his judgments upon character. The drift of his influence was away from metaphysical speculation, for though he had a clear head in argument he was not particularly fitted to follow complicated trains of abstract reasoning. His days and nights were spent in reading and in long, leisurely, laughing, intimate talks. It has been said of Edward Fitzgerald that his friendships were more like loves, and that might also be said of Lytton Strachey.

His influence, especially upon his younger contemporaries, was to fix their attention on emotions and relations between human beings. He was a master of what may be called psychological gossip, the kind which treats friends as diagrams of the human species and ranges over the past and fiction as well as history, in search of whatever illustrates this or that side of human nature. He was writing a good deal of verse too, some of it of a ribald kind, the rest emotional, and marked by that intellectual elaboration we associate with the metaphysical school of poets, the seventeenth century poets, or the classic impetuosity of such verses as Pope's 'Abelard and Héloise'.

Just as his taste in prose was towards a Gallic clarity and the Latin elements in our culture, towards the amenity and composed vigour of the eighteenth century, his taste in poetry inclined him towards the Elizabethans and their immediate successors. He loved in poetry things extreme and dazzling bright, the golden moments of emotion that shoot up and spatter the skies—though he always kept his eye on the falling stick. The poetry which was wit's forge and fire-blast, meaning's press and screw, enraptured him.

I have little doubt that the change in the diction of Rupert Brooke's verse was due to the inflection of Lytton Strachey's enthusiasm for Donne and seventeenth century poetry, and perhaps to those poems of his own he used to read at Cambridge to his friends. I will quote two of his love poems which belong to a series which records an emotional experience, because they reveal a side of Lytton Strachey which the irony and detachment of his writings have hidden from most of his readers. The first is called 'Knowledge', the second 'The Exhumation'.

KNOWLEDGE

If you could look into the hidden place
   Wherein my soul's remembrance dwells alone,
Methinks you'd say, with wonder in your face,
   'How strange have been the things that you have known!'

For I have seen in half-extinguished eyes
   The dumb assuagements of immortal grief,
Infinitudes of exquisite surprise,
   Looks beyond love, and tears beyond belief.

And subtle transmutations I have seen
   Upon a dreaming face subtly unfold,
As when in autumn heavens purpureal green
   Gradually melts to opalescent gold.

And I have heard the guttural voice of lust
   Moaning upon the boundaries of thought,
Extraordinary as the bloody dust
   That smears the enormous mouth of Juggernaut.

I have explored despairs and hopes and joys
   More secret than the zone of Proserpine,
Or those immaculate whisperings in the boy's
   Soft somnolent ears, Endymion's, when divine

Over Idaean forests swept the moon.
   And I have felt the unknown Calumeth
Upon my brow come dropping, and the swoon
   Over my soul of memories dim as death.

Yet have all these strange things more common grown
   To me than the dead leaf at the year's fall.
I count not strange these things that I have known;
   For I have known the strangest thing of all.

Sept. 1907

What strange moment in his emotional life is there recorded I
do not know.

THE EXHUMATION

Oh, what rash fancy did your spirit move
To resurrect my long-expirèd love?
What was there in that corpse that you should break
So much thick stone asunder for its sake?
Ah, did your heart not fail you, when the light
To that assured eternity of night
Put a quick period, and the heedless sun
Undid at once what all those years had done?
For, at this strange new last unhallowed birth
My dead desire left the womb of earth
Arrayed, not as an infant, but a bride,
No less magnificent than when it died.
Such lustrous eyes no eyes had ever seen
Since those of the embalm'd Arthurian queen
Conquered in death that conqueror of old,
Nor such fresh roses and amazing gold.
Yes, it was easy to forget that grace
Adorned no more than a sepulchral face;
And who would dare prognosticate a kiss
Plucked from that mouth were anything but bliss?
But when you stooped your lips down, and at last
Touched—oh, touched what?—did you not shrink aghast
To see in one swift second disappear
That vision, like the body of Guinevere,
And all the rich alembic of my lust
Turn in a moment to a little dust?

Perhaps these verses may surprise you as coming from him.

Close readers of his works will not, however, I think, be
surprised at the side these poems reveal. They will have noticed
here and there his sympathy with what is extreme and open
in the expression of emotion, and in the last large subject that
he chose for a book, *Elizabeth and Essex*, that is clearly seen.
The Strachey fans were stupid about *Elizabeth and Essex*; 'the
intellectuals', like the great naïve public, wanted him to do the
same thing over and over again, they wanted to go on enjoying
his irony playing round historic figures, hitherto beyond the
reach of irreverence and above suspicion.

The duality of his temperament found a parallel in certain

physical characteristics. He spoke with two voices. The one tiny as that of the gnat in *Alice in Wonderland*; the other grave and deep. The first voice added a spice to his quick interjections, puncturing pomposity or checking impertinence. I remember, soon after he had grown that long reddish beard which added so much to the dignity of his appearance, a lady asking him 'Oh, Mr Strachey, tell me, when you go to bed, do you keep that beard of yours inside or outside the blankets?' It was in the gnat-like voice that he replied 'Come and see!'

But in reading Racine or the Elizabethan dramatists (which he did admirably and with great feeling) or at moments when he expressed indignation rather than contempt, it was his sombre and majestic tones you heard. There was a similar contrast in his demeanour; an extreme passivity bordering on lassitude was apt to be broken by the most fantastic gesticulation when he repudiated some enormity or hailed an extravagance that delighted him.

How long the pauses were between his books! He was not an ambitious man—at least, not after he had proved both to himself and his friends that the gifts they had divined in him were really there. Other feelings were far stronger in him than ambition. He did not like characters in whom ambition took control of personal relations and destroyed detachment. He had a keen eye, as his studies in human nature show, for the fantastic antics and morose stupidities that ambition inspires. He did not even like, though he excused and admired (you remember his *Florence Nightingale*) the egotism of ruthless devotion which is kin to ambition. His books are surprisingly accurate, considering how attractive as 'a note' every significant, though perhaps not well authenticated, fact must have been to him. His fine sense for what is entertaining lent his work an apparent slightness that concealed the pains he had taken in writing it. This sense of what is entertaining supported his instincts as an artist, and when writing *Queen Victoria* it directed his path through the forest of facts from 1817 to 1901.

He was determined that at every turn in that path something should beguile us. Without this unerring sense of what is entertaining he would never have found his way. Where, too, he showed himself a craftsman, was in conducting his narrative (and this is seen in his short biographies also) so that we do not even miss a thorough treatment of the large unaccommodating historic facts, in front of which a lesser artist in biography would have felt bound to detain us. The miracle is that though there are omissions these are not felt as gaps. What pains he must have taken to maintain that beguiling smoothness! How deftly he used the indirect method!

'The history of the Victorian Age will never be written: we know too much about it', he wrote in the Preface to *Eminent Victorians*. ' . . . It is not by the direct method of a scrupulous narrative that the explorer of the past can hope to depict that singular epoch. If he is wise he will adopt a subtler strategy.'

And he added: 'It has been my purpose to illustrate rather than to explain.' Now, since history is chiefly concerned with causality (it is this preoccupation which distinguishes the historian proper), Lytton Strachey was a painter of the past and a biographer, not a historian. Note the adjective 'singular' in the phrase he applied to the Victorian Age, that 'singular epoch'. Nobody before had seen it just like that. The Victorian Age had been lashed again and again by indignant economic historians, and almost as fiercely as by its own children, Carlyle and Ruskin; but its prestige was still imposing. When Lytton Strachey looked at it with calm amazement, many twentieth century readers discovered that they too had moved, half unconsciously, so far from the standards and convictions of the Victorian Age that the word 'singular', with its ironic inflection, described what they felt about it themselves.

Now amazement, though an enjoyable condition of mind, cannot be prolonged and continue to please, and, when maintained for the sake of flattering the sense of superiority which may accompany it, it becomes both contemptible and tiresome. We are now heartily sick of the amused and surprised smiles of any scribbling whippersnapper who chooses to turn his face towards the great Victorians. But that is no blame to Lytton Strachey, nor can he be held responsible for the cheap effects of those who have imitated him without his 'subtler strategy', his careful curiosity, his perspicuous serenity and—I am coming to that—his moral passion. A writer's imitators, as Macaulay knew, are more destructive of his reputation than his sourest critics; but, however regrettable, these results are proof of originality and fascination. Lytton Strachey's importance can be measured by his having both focused and intensified our consciousness of the differences between nineteenth and twentieth century modes of thinking and feeling, and in having changed, by his dangerous example, the methods of popular biography. That influence alone would have secured him a place in the history of literature, even if his own work did not possess the finish and freshness which preserves.

Like most original and influential men, he was bold. His boldness was effortless, and because he admired and firmly believed in certain qualities in human nature and in certain attitudes of mind, he was also the natural foe of ideals and patterns of virtue which tend to brow-beat the qualities he valued and loved. The public thought he was a frivolous and detached ironist, but he was much more of a moralist. Only in writing he avoided carefully, for aesthetic reasons, the portentous frown of the earnest writer. He did not believe in the Christian religion, and he was one of the few English writers about the past—Gibbon was another—who have allowed scepticism to colour their view of believers.

Lytton Strachey was like Voltaire in three respects: he thought beliefs absurd in others which he thought absurd in himself, and he was convinced that as long as men continued to believe absurdities they would continue to commit atrocities. As a moralist he believed that *surtout point de zèle*, except against zealots, was a trustworthy guide to right living and right judgment. The public thought this was only his naughty relish for poking destructive fun—but then the public are so immoral they do not recognise a moralist unless he bears the conventional insignia about him.

There is, by the by, not nearly so much destructive irony, and a great deal more sympathy, in his work than is generally supposed. I could quote many passages of delicate sensitive sympathy with those whose outlook upon life he did not share. (Recall the pages on Newman in *Eminent Victorians* and *passim* his fairness to the far from charming but honourable figure of the Prince Consort in *Queen Victoria*.)

Seldom has a born writer, who, as the essay on 'English Letter Writers' now shows, matured so early, had so long a period of incubating: he was thirty-seven when *Eminent Victorians* appeared. This was partly due to ill-health, but perhaps even more to the warring of those two tendencies in him—the romantic and the rational. He did not know what he wanted most to do, or, rather, he was uncertain what he could do best. He would have wished, I think, to write poetic drama. His sense of form, his passionate pre-occupation with human nature, made drama extremely attractive to him. Elizabeth and Essex was a subject which had called to him in youth.

Mr Francis Birrell, in an excellent essay which he contributed to *La Revue Hebdomadaire* in July 1932, pointed out that Strachey's *Elizabeth and Essex* is almost a sketch for a play. The long meditations attributed to Elizabeth, to Essex, to Bacon, and Cecil, are monologues inspired by those of the Elizabethan drama, where the protagonist often occupies the stage alone, delivering in poetry the passions and perplexities which divide his soul. Like Antony, Essex leaves and returns to his Queen; like Antony he dies a violent death. The passage, so carefully weighed, with which the book ends, where Cecil is seen at his writing table, brooding over the future of England and the destiny of his own house, is also an invention borrowed from the Elizabethan stage. Does not *Antony and Cleopatra* close with the triumph of Octavius, *Hamlet* with the crowning of Fortinbras? It is well to keep this parallel in mind in judging the book. It disappointed some of Strachey's admirers because, like all admirers, they wanted him to repeat himself. But I believe that as time goes on *Elizabeth and Essex* will be rated much higher. It contains some of the finest and most imaginative prose he ever wrote.

'Human beings', he wrote, 'are too important to be treated as mere symptoms of the past. They have a value which is independent of any temporal process—which is eternal, and must be felt for its own sake. The art of biography seems to have fallen on evil times in England. We have had, it is true, a few masterpieces, but we have never had, like the French, a great biographical tradition; we have had no Fontenelles and Condorcets with their incomparable *éloges*, compressing into a few shining pages the manifold existences of men. With us, the most delicate and humane of all the branches of the art of writing has been relegated to the journeymen of letters. . . .'

To preserve a becoming brevity which excludes everything redundant but nothing that is significant, that, surely is the first duty of the biographer. The second, no less surely, is to maintain his own freedom of spirit.

It was in this, 'the most delicate and humane of all the branches of the art of writing', that he excelled, and he did so, apart from his gifts as a writer and story-teller, thanks to 'maintaining his own freedom of spirit'. There lay his originality when he began to write. It was the custom of our biographers to curb in themselves 'freedom of spirit'. They deliberately obliterated their own attitude towards life, either adopting for the time that of the man about whom they were writing or a nondescript point of view supposed to be equivalent to 'impartiality'. The lives of Conservatives were written by Conservatives, of Liberals by Liberals; those of religious leaders and reformers by writers who either shared their convictions or pretended to do so. These books might have great merits, but they could not have those of a work of art. Take, for example, Morley's *Life of Gladstone*: no one would guess from that book that Lord Morley was an ardent rationalist. His rationalism must have made many of Gladstone's judgments and emotions, and much of his behaviour, appear fantastic to him: though he might not cease to admire, Morley's admiration must have been often tinged with irony or amazement. But he was on his honour 'as a biographer' to let none of this appear in his book. A work of art cannot be created under such conditions. To Lytton Strachey biography was interpretation, and therefore the record, not only of facts, but of the biographer's deepest response to them. There could be no genuine focus otherwise, no vital principle of selection. When he says 'human beings are too important to be treated as mere symptoms of the past' he gives us the clue to his own sense of proportion. His preoccupation was with human nature itself, and only incidentally with the causes of events or of changes. These he had often to deal with in order to tell the story, and admirably he did so: witness his masterly summary of the Oxford Movement, or of the causes of the tardy change in the Liberal Government towards Gordon and the Sudan. But it is upon the effect of temperament and character on events that he invariably fixes our attention, or, again, upon the effect of events upon character, as he has shown with such skill in his *Queen Victoria*. He fulfilled the task of the biographer as Johnson defined it.

Lytton Strachey was 51 when he died. Serious as the loss to Literature was admitted to be, it was greater than at once appeared. It is likely that we have been robbed of his finest book. The poet and the novelist usually repeat themselves after maturity; their work is so dependent upon inspiration, invention and emotion, things which age slowly takes away. They may keep their skill, their insight, but they see and record for us little that they have not used before. But of the man of letters it is much truer to say 'ripeness is all'. In the work of the biographer and historian knowledge and judgment are relatively much more important, and until lassitude sets in, and with lassitude that finished garrulity and serene laxity which are its fatal signs, years only add to his knowledge and widen his view. I am sure, alas, that in Lytton Strachey's case the best was yet to come. But what an artist he had already proved himself!

AUSONIUS

1933

I HAVE two counsellors who pull me different ways. One this
way: 'Why do you look with such a bland indifference on
the present? Dead poets, novelists, cranks, dead philosophers, scoundrels, statesmen, can rouse you to even a controversial pitch of animation, but you tackle contemporaries with
a sigh of boredom.' (A murmured protest from me.)

'At least you'll admit that when I mention the French
Revolution you are alive in a moment, while at the word
"Russia" apathy wraps you in a cloud. The uncultured—yes,
the people who mostly read the papers, letting old news (what
else is history?) take a poor after-chance, have a sounder sense
of proportion than that. Their curiosity, for what it's worth, is
directed upon life, not still-life. In August 1914 I overheard
an elderly gentleman inveighing heavily at luncheon against
the conduct of the war. It was not, as yet, patriotic to abuse
our Government and generals; his indignation was resented
till it was discovered that he had been talking of the Crimean
War.

'You remind me of him. I should like to hold your inquisitive
nose on to the whizzing wheel of Today. If that takes the skin
off, so much the better—and the better, too, in the long run,
for your work.'

To this friend I reply: 'One writes on what one can, not
necessarily on what is urgent.' Yet he makes me uneasy, and
adolescently ambitious too. Perhaps, I think after a talk with
him—perhaps I really have some contribution to make. What
a stimulating prospect, what an infernal responsibility!

But my second counsellor soothes me. He talks like this:
'You are a literary man; you should write for literary people
not for those who are confined to the moment—in a great

measure through the inferiority of their faculties. Literature is an important part of life; taste is a high morality.' In this connection he, too, has a war-time anecdote to tell. It concerns a young professor of literature who, accosted by one of those tiresome women with feathers and asked why he was not fighting to save civilisation, replied, 'I am the civilisation they are trying to save.'

I should, this friend insists, take home that significant retort; it's not for me to influence events or join the mellay of contemporary ideas. The present is only the last inch of a long mile, and no more interesting to thought than many a one behind it; and if scholars and aesthetes should be faithless to their preoccupations, then the present—for all—would be emptier and more common. 'Never try to keep pace with things,' he repeated when last we met, 'make them revolve round your private focus. And try to write well; no one listens for more than three days to those who cannot write. What is your next subject?'

'I write—and am listened to for *one*,' said I, knowing that I was being modest, 'and next Sunday my subject is—Ausonius.' He smiled approval. But he may not like my treatment of it: the other counsellor still pulls.

Mr Mackail, in his foreword to Mr Blakeney's verse translation of the *Mosella* of Ausonius says that it can be read on its own account with pleasure. This is authoritative; though, for my part, I should have said—chiefly with *historic interest*, rising here and there to literary enjoyment by mild degrees. Of the poetic merit of the original I cannot judge. Mr Mackail has written in his *Latin Literature* that the *Mosella* unites 'Virgilian rhythm and diction with a new romantic sense of the beauties of nature'—new for those days and hundreds of years to come. He summarises thus the charming impressions which its descriptive passages have left upon his mind:

. . . the liquid lapse of waters, the green, wavering reflections, the belt of crisp sand by the water's edge, and the long weeds swaying with the stream, the gleaming gravel-beds under the water, with their patches of moss and the quick fishes darting hither and thither over them; or the oftener quoted and not less beautiful lines where he breaks into rapture over the sunset colouring of stream and bank, and the glassy water, where, at evening, all the hills waver and the vine-tendril shakes and the grape-bunches swell in the crystal mirror. In virtue of this poem Ausonius ranks not merely as the last, or all but the last, of Latin, but as the first of French poets.

This is a fruitful idea—to take a river for a theme; or, for that matter, any mountain, forest, town. I marvelled, after reading this old poem on the Moselle, that the example had not been followed by later poets. What a resource it might prove today for many a poet who, finding his lyric impulse waning, now turns, without the smallest aptitude for dramatic construction, to writing blank-verse plays; tales booked for oblivion. What opportunities such a theme as, say, the history of the New Forest offers him, not only for natural description, but for human drama, from when huts first blazed to make a hunting ground for Rufus and the arrow struck him in the desert he had made, down to the days when charabancs hourly arrive and cosy, rosy homes hide themselves among the trees; or, say (for a poet with a turn for social satire), the story of the Sussex fishing-village of Brighthelmstone, or the Thames.

On such themes a poet could use his gifts for drawing men and painting passions without a stage; and behind it all would he not have the contrast between Permanence and Change?

Ausonius interweaves associations with descriptions and river-life with mythology. It is loosely done, and with that tolerance of tangential references to which the classic long-tailed metaphor is itself a witness. We are often led far from the river; sometimes by discourse upon the table virtues of its various fish, or upon the luxury of those great mansions, with their colonnades and winter and summer apartments, which boats and barges continually pass; now standing 'low 'mid well-watered fields', now 'on a hill that hangs towering above the stream'. (We might be floating, as we read, past Nuneham, Cliveden, Taplow Court.)

And then the bathing! Ausonius has watched the bathers, sweaty from the hot-room baths, scorning the proper plunging-pools, rush to the running water. There are spots along the river where, he says, the stranger might think himself at Baiae,

> So great
> The lure of all this beauty, all this charm.

He likes to imagine nymphs in the river—of course, pursued by satyrs, and

> sliding thro' the hands
> Of these unartful swimmers, who, deceived,
> Clutch at those slippery bodies, and in place
> Of limbs embrace nought but the buxom flood.

'Buxom' is an adjective of Mr Blakeney's invention; the Latin is *liquidosque fluctus*. His own suits the Boucher-like picture, yet I would have preferred 'the yielding stream'.

Ausonius (he was a Christian—well, in the sense Macaulay was) adds slyly that it is no sin to speak thus of what no eye has seen; yet one feels he wishes that he could have found any excuse but that. The interlude recalls the bland sophistication of those times, when the minds of cultivated men were half lit by the solemn moonrise of Christianity, half gilded by the setting sun of paganism. There was a twilight time of tolerance in Gaul.

They say that till the eighteenth century travelling was never again so easy and frequent; and the ruling classes, since they could visit each other, found country-life far pleasanter than that of the towns. As power slipped from them they spent, too, more time and money on their lovely villas. Ausonius belonged to that class; in an autobiographical poem he has left a sketch of his career:

My father, a physician, bore the same name as myself. Bazas was his native place; my mother was of Aeduan descent. I myself am a native of Bordeaux. Listen to the record of my days. From early youth I gave myself to the study of literature (*grammaticum studium*) and of rhetoric; and though I frequented the law courts, teaching was my chosen business, and as a teacher my reputation stood high. Thirty years later I gave up my professional duties, as I had received an imperial request to undertake the task of instructing Gratian, the Emperor's young son. Greater tutors there have been, but to none has been granted the privilege of teaching a nobler pupil. And today he is Master of the World. He made me *comes* (a Privy Counsellor) and *quaestor*, crowning my career with the Prefectship of Gaul, Libya, and Italy. Finally I became Consul.

Culture and birth admitted to the high enclosure at the top of this old, broad, powerful civilisation—culture as Ausonius has just shown. To those like him that civilisation must have seemed too ripe and far-embracing ever to fall, though it had sometimes rocked then. Yet it was doomed—and how quickly it was to disintegrate! The year he died (395) the Roman world split; 'a dozen years later the whole of France was overswept by the barbarian invaders; Aquitaine became a Visigothic kingdom'. Continuous pressure from without at last had fatally shaken that equilibrium within, on which civilisation—for all its seemingly inexhaustible material resources—depends.

What then results is like paralysis: the smooth, strong limbs lie there with all their intricate arrangement of sinews, muscles, arteries; they twitch, but they cannot be moved. Then they decay; and men struggle to maintain a life they would have thought a dog's before. The poetry of Ausonius was more interesting to me as having been written on the eve of that crash than for its literary merits. It seemed so modern; it showed that men, when nothing can be done, do not believe the worst can happen.

GALSWORTHY

1933

ON the morning of George Moore's death on Saturday, 21st January, I wrote a brief notice for the *Sunday Times*, and that evening, through the B.B.C., I spoke my 'hail and farewell' to him as an artist. These were not estimates of his work—they could not be; they were gestures of admiration which I could make with ease and sincerity.

On 31st January 1933, an author of far wider fame died, John Galsworthy, and it falls to me to comment also upon him. But from me commentary in this case has to differ from a funeral oration; it has to be criticism, and some of it inevitably seems ungenerous. It soothes my embarrassment, however, to reflect that during these few last days so many have read so many times so many things written in his praise, that already there is no need to muffle the voice of an *advocatus diaboli*. Sooner or later, before every canonisation was completed, he had to be heard. Why should he not then speak at once? At any rate I leave my apology at that. My eye has already noticed among these eulogies such phrases as 'his brush is that of Rembrandt, not that of Michael Angelo': encouraged, the Devil's Advocate proceeds.

Among his world-famous contemporaries the case of Galsworthy is most curious in that there was with him a wider gap between merit and reputation than with the others. It was not that his merits were small, but that his reputation was colossal. I am not speaking of sales or popularity—these we know bear an uncertain relation to achievement—but of fervid admiration, both here and abroad. He was a very good writer of the second class who had the renown of a master, a genius, an artist. How did it happen? He did nothing himself to foster such exaggerations; his career was one of exemplary detachment. The

Presidency of The Pen Club, whose members frequently entertain distinguished foreigners, may have helped in some measure towards his obtaining the Nobel Prize, but how little that must have counted, those who have travelled recently on the Continent, loitered by foreign railway stalls or in foreign bookshops, talked with Germans, Frenchmen, or Scandinavians about English authors, are in a position to understand. No pardonable misapprehensions on the part of bewildered and gratified visitors as to the representative status of The Pen Club can account for those piles of translations, or for the universal alacrity with which it is assumed abroad that if you are interested in literature you must think Galsworthy a great writer.

The foreigner supposes that when he reads Galsworthy he is understanding the English at last, that when he follows the Forsytes he is watching the very pulse of the machine. His instant response to figures, so emphatically projected as types, conceals from him their lack of individual vitality, and the author's attitude towards them (that tone of a severe and scrupulous judge) prevents him from noticing that Galsworthy's satire invariably relents towards sentiment. Yet the foreigner concluded that here at last was an unflinching dissector of the propertied philistine backbone of England! Even MM. Legouis and Cazamian praise Galsworthy for 'boldness' and depth. It is hard to convince foreigners that in the days when they were content with the certainly perfunctory diagnosis that all Englishmen were 'mad', they were in a way nearer to truth than after reading *The Forsyte Saga*. That diagnosis was at least a pot-shot at the core of erratic emotional independence beneath conventional repressions, at that inner—not external—spontaneity of feeling which Galsworthy's characters notably fail to reflect.

One peculiarity of the Englishman is that you can so seldom count on him being true to type. Yet one of the most general characteristics of the Galsworthian picture of England is that everybody, even the artist-rebels (who by the by are neither *real* rebels nor *real* artists), behaves and speaks typically. The

element of the unexpected is what I miss in the characters both
in his plays and in his novels. Again, that strong family cohesion,
the Joint-Stock Company spirit, which, in spite of defections
from it, is the soul of *The Forsyte Saga*, is really more characteristic of France than England—perhaps this explains why,
there, it was so readily recognised. Forsyte groups no doubt
exist, but in no country is indifference to family unity more
common than in England.

There was one circumstance that ought to have enlightened
readers abroad who hailed Galsworthy as an unsparing critic
of the conventional possessive Englishman: his immense popularity at home. No writer in that kind who really hits the mark
is effusively and at once accepted in his own country. Galsworthy drew propertied Englishmen not as they are, but as they
can stand seeing themselves at moments when they are prepared to admit, with a humility which hardly perturbs them,
that they certainly have grave faults. No Englishman objects
to being depicted as an obstinate oak of a man, gnarled and set
in prejudice, putting forth perhaps in old age some tender
sunlit leaves, or to being described as pig-headed, a philistine,
dominated by a ruthless sense of material values, for those are
not his radical faults, not those which make him wince if they
are probed. No Irishman objects to being satirised as a feckless
fellow, no one's enemy but his own, as one too imaginative to
act, too spontaneous to look ahead. But if an Irishman touches
the real national defects, lack of moral courage and cruelty, it
will be some time before he is hailed in Erin as an author of
whom his countrymen may well be proud. Frenchmen feel
quite friendly to their own novelists, who depict them as
volatile and lascivious, but hardly any talent will make a writer
popular in France who mocks French stinginess and blind
vindictive self-assertion.

English faults have not such precise abusive names, nevertheless they are disgusting. They can be indicated: an incurable
determination in the face of truth, honour, art, to have things
both ways (the nearest curse-word for this is hypocrisy, though

that is far too crude), and an impenetrable self-complacency—smugness for short, smugness moral and intellectual. The popularity of Galsworthy in England ought to have suggested to foreigners that his exposure of English character and society did not really go deep. But did not he lash smugness in the Forsytes? Yes, but—here speaks the Devil's Advocate—this exposure was not entirely free from it. He yielded to the desire to have things both ways; to champion passion, for instance, yet call it Love of Beauty. He defined Irene and the part she played in the Forsyte drama as 'a concretion of disturbing Beauty impinging on a possessive world'. He wanted to envisage the struggle as one between *Beauty* and Possessiveness. It made it nobler. But he would have done 'Beauty', and incidentally drawn his artist-rebels, far better if he had recognised the real nature of the struggle—possessiveness versus sex.

His predominant characteristics as a dramatist were an admirable clarity in construction and an effective, but in the end disappointing, under-statement of emotion in dialogue; he worked colloquial inexpressiveness on the stage too hard. His characters were never complex, his situations definite, his intentions clear. In those respects he resembles Brieux. Both dramatists were essentially demonstrators; both found inspiration in social problems. In both a love of justice created an atmosphere peculiar to their plays.

His dramatic aim seemed to be not to make us live in his people but to make us fair-minded towards them. The result was that though the power to rouse indignation and pity was within his scope, tragic feeling and free comedy were not. It was as though he was satisfied once he had done equal justice to everybody, although he had not done complete, or, if you will, artistic or poetic, justice to anybody. His characters were drawn with admirable clearness, but he seemed more interested in them as 'cases' than as individuals. The temptation to which he yielded as a creator was to think more about the representative value of his characters than about character itself. It is all to the good that a play or novel should have a 'moral'.

That is to say, that it should have a bearing upon life as we have observed it, and that an author's mind should be full of the general woe or joy of the world. But only on condition that when once he sits down to write his interest in his people exceeds everything else. It was in this respect that, though we could still honour him as a reformer, Galsworthy failed.

He never wrote a better play than his first. *The Silver Box* was a modest little realistic drama, perfectly contrived to bring out an ironic contrast and a social moral. He often showed that the Law was an ass, and cruel at that, but though he did so afterwards by more violent appeals to our commiseration for its victims, he did not achieve his end so well in *Justice* or *Escape*. *The Pigeon* stands high among his plays because in it he dropped that craving to be fair, and allowed all his tender nature to rush in welcome, not in pity, towards a character of his creating. There may be qualities more inspiring in human nature, but there are none more moving to contemplate than an unalterable natural kindness. The pigeon himself was an embodiment of it. Galsworthy knew how little this loving-kindness can achieve.

Wellwyn was not a saver of souls, he could not make wasters pull themselves together. He was not interested in people because they were citizens or immortal souls, but because he could not help liking them very much as they were—even when he wished they were different. To his exasperated daughter he seemed 'a sickly sentimentalist'. He was shocked by misery and unhappiness, being equable and gay himself, but he could not be disgusted with human beings however they behaved. Though the Wellwyns are no use in righting wrongs or putting things straight; though philanthropists and reformers agree that they do harm by 'indiscriminate charity', what they do give —and they are the only people who give it to those most starved for it—is affection, in which there is neither forethought nor afterthought, neither patronage nor criticism.

There was a good deal of Wellwyn in Galsworthy himself, but he wanted first to be sensible and a just critic of social life; the Wellwyn in him, so to speak, only trickled out in a sentimentality which often spoilt his work or made him concentrate too much on rousing pity. Mr Edward Shanks has said that 'his main characteristic was zealousness in the cause of the underdog, tempered with a wide charity for the top-dog—a combination which to most of us is impossible'. That was the Wellwyn in him struggling for free expression: emotionally he had to let people off, even Soames (his triumph in characterisation) in the end. Mr Shanks is wrong in thinking such division of sympathy is rare. It is found, for example, in every good magistrate. Art demands that a writer should find his centre, or that he should write at any rate at the moment from some unchecked impulse in himself. Galsworthy's mind was full of checks and glosses. He wanted to combine the passionate sympathiser with the calmness of the judge. Very, very hard to do. I have used a phrase to place him, 'a very good writer of the second class', which only sounds offensive because the currency of praise has been so absurdly debased, since in his work the sympathetic magistrate strikes me as having triumphed over the intuitive artist.

WILLIAM SOMERSET MAUGHAM

1934

NOVELISTS may be said to enjoy a first-rate prestige when their works both delight the many and satisfy the discriminating few. Some have attained it by first impressing the few; others by first capturing the many. I have noticed that reputations which spread outwards from a narrow circle tend to die away at the centre as their circumference widens; so suspicious are the few of contemporary success. 'Can we have been right?' they ask themselves. 'Why, he's popular!' It is safer, and also perhaps a surer guarantee of lasting prestige, to conquer the big common world first, as Dickens and Balzac did, and afterwards to win the reluctant admiration of those who regard themselves as bestowing real fame, and whose respect is indeed an absolutely necessary ingredient in it.

The development of Somerset Maugham's reputation has been on the whole from without inwards, and that is one reason why his position in the world of letters is now so sure. It is true that he actually began as an author for the few with a realistic story of slum life, *Liza of Lambeth* (1897), but his name became so soon associated with popular money-making plays that this was forgotten. *Liza of Lambeth* was the fruit of his experience of maternity cases in poverty-stricken London after he had taken his medical degree at St. Thomas's Hospital. It was controlled by that iron kind of pity which the intellectuals of the 'nineties particularly admired. They accepted him at once as an author destined to climb the long, lonely road to eminence, unrefreshed by lavish royalties, uncheered by popular applause. His friends were of the Yellow Book; his reputation confined to the few. He studied patiently the art of fine phrasing, but in vain; since for him the natural approach to good style was a more direct one than that of aping others who had attained it.

Presently (I remember this well) he was hailed by the papers as the 'most fortunate young man in London': he had three highly successful plays running at the same time! And this had happened only to Barrie before him. Certainly, it was no surprise that he should appear as a dramatist, for he had already written plays, one of which had been performed inconspicuously in Berlin, the other by the Stage Society. Such *succés d'estime* had been in keeping with the reputation of the author of *Liza*, but this resounding, blatant triumph was a different matter. And his successes went on snowballing up! *Lady Frederick, Jack Straw, Mrs Dot, The Explorer*, were followed by *Penelope, Smith* and other plays in rapid succession. This young doctor who had had to look at every shilling before he spent it, whom an innate passion for observation and reflection had slowly drawn into the life of letters and who, finding himself an author, had been at once preoccupied with problems of style, had also been employing his time in writing popular plays! (He had found, by the by, the usual difficulty in getting them accepted, till *Lady Frederick* started managers clamouring for those they had rejected.) Now he had suddenly become a rich man with an elegant house in Mayfair and a place of some prominence in London society, moving in it, however (and this is important in our diagnosis), with the reserve and detachment of a professional man of letters. The immediate effect of this transformation was to obscure his reputation with the few as a serious writer. He became identified with his successes as a popular playwright. Those early plays which made his name and fortune were well-constructed and lively, but they had little interest for the critical. They were 'telling' enough, but they told nothing new. They were just cynical enough to make the sentimental-worldly think themselves tough-minded while they were enjoying them, and just brilliant enough to satisfy a London audience's far from exacting standard of wit. I did not myself believe in his gift for comedy till I saw it later in *Caroline* and *Home and Beauty*. How completely, before the war, his name had become associated with the production of able but commercial plays I can illustrate by my own reactions.

I made Mr Maugham's acquaintance in 1914. We were attached to the same section of the Red Cross Ambulances which were sent over to France just after the first battle of Ypres. Apart from the immediate pleasure of his company, I, who either from curiosity or admiration, had eagerly sought out many writers, was not interested at finding myself thrown together with him. A scene in a little bedroom at Malo near Dunkirk comes back to me: a thick roll of proofs had arrived for him; he had corrected them and the long strips were lying on the bed. They were evidently the proofs of a novel. Now, although I was short of something to read, my interest in them was confined to noticing how very few corrections he had made. When I remarked on it, he replied that he always went over his work carefully before he sent it to the printer.

'Ah', I thought, 'he's as business-like as a novelist as he is as a playwright. The itch for perfection doesn't trouble him; the adequate will do. I suppose the book will sell.' And these were the proofs of *Of Human Bondage*! A novel which, together with *The Old Wives' Tale*, *Farewell to Arms*, *Kipps*, *Babbitt*, and a few others, will float on the stream of time when the mass of modern realistic fiction is sediment at the bottom.

It may not seem at first sight so surprising that Somerset Maugham should have won back the admiration of intellectuals as that he should have kept that of the common reader. He has neither the temperament, nor the outlook on life that comports with popularity. He is not good-natured, effusive or optimistic. His estimates of human-nature are pretty grim. He is inclined to think of life as a game played against an adversary bound to win, even when a player makes his moves with the most circumspect selfishness. This shows that the public, to its credit, appreciates a good story, even though the spirit which informs the tale may be far from meeting its usual demands. Who, after all, has enjoyed a wider or more lasting popularity as a story-teller than Maupassant? And who was more pessimistic? But such a writer must be one who *can* tell a story, who himself prefers stories with a point and can convey in immediately intelligible words whatever he describes.

Somerset Maugham possesses all the gifts essential in a popular realist. He has a sense of what is widely interesting, because, like Maupassant, he is as much a man of the world as he is an artist—otherwise his themes would never have been so generally intelligible; while at his best he can tell a story as well as any man alive or dead. Witness 'The Alien Corn', or 'The Human Element', or 'The Out-Station' in that collection he has called *The Casuarina Tree*. How perfectly he held in it the balance in the deadly quarrel between two isolated civil servants, between a 'snob' and a 'cad'! And what stories could be better told than 'Rain' or that of the disillusioned but sordidly contented ex-medical student and opium smuggler near the end of *The Gentleman in the Parlour*, or the poignant incident of the trapped English traitor with his German wife, in that series of secret service stories, *Ashenden, or The British Agent*? Whenever experience has suggested a subject of lasting significance and thoroughly suited to his own temperament, Somerset Maugham has treated it like a master.

In his novels his hand is apt to falter towards the end, though *Cakes and Ale* is a notable exception. From the first pages to the last, *Cakes and Ale* is a model of construction, and its theme presented a particularly difficult problem. The intention in it was twofold; to depict two characters to the life, a novelist and his wife, Driffield and Rosie, and at the same time to examine without mercy the manner in which exaggerated literary reputations are artificially stimulated, to study the kind of people who increase their own importance by battening on an author whose fame they help to create, and how they handle to that end the *machine à la gloire*, so powerful today. Rosie is one of those characters whose worth survives the corrosion of the author's scepticism with regard to human goodness. She is not, needless to say, an exalted type. What he loves in her is an unadorned physical beauty and a human earthly soundness. That he can trust. And when he has created her in her softly-glowing charm and delicious honest kindliness, how one respects him for not killing her in order that we should take leave of her in the pathetic and becoming light of early death! The final appearance of Rosie in New York as a game old bridge-playing woman of seventy, still in love with life, was no doubt a shock. But what a salutary shock! Age destroys beauty slowly, death suddenly; it is well to learn that this is the only difference. It is sentimental to wish the 'pilgrim soul' in Rosie had been snuffed out in order that we might have escaped seeing her old, fat, pink, made-up, and happy. The beauty that has been, has been—in either case.

It is impossible to avoid the adjective cynical in an article on Somerset Maugham, but he is not cynical about Rosie or about the passionate affection which united that Jewish family in 'The Alien Corn' who hoped so ardently and vainly to be taken for Gentiles, or about—well, I could make a long list, not only of characters, but incidents, towards which his attitude is far from cynical—pitiful rather, with an artist's pity which makes the naïve reader think that he is moved while the brute of an author remains stony-hearted. He does not understand that he is so deeply touched himself only because the story-teller shed no tears.

There is an aside in *Cakes and Ale* where the author remarks that the one great advantage of being a writer is that you can rid yourself of painful experience by projecting it on paper; it suggests a core of sensibility which the observant will perceive behind Somerset Maugham's wary and aloof attitude as an observer.

His response to life is that of a sensitive man whom painful experience taught early to grow a thick skin. His character-drawing is that of one who does not yield himself readily to impulses of affection, admiration, generosity, who is on guard against being the dupe of a show of these qualities in others,

c

and suspicious of their genuineness in himself. Remember that people are hard because they have, or think they have, borne as much as they can be asked to bear. There is a significant passage in which he speaks for himself in *The Human Element*. One of the characters, whom he hardly knows, suddenly blurts out the words, 'I'm so desperately unhappy'.

'He said it without warning', the narrator continues. 'He obviously meant it. There was in his tone a sort of gasp. It might very well have been a sob. I cannot describe what a shock it was to me to hear him say those words. I felt as you do when you turn a corner of the street and on a sudden a great blast of wind meets you, takes your breath away, and nearly blows you off your feet. It was so unexpected. After all I hardly knew the fellow. We were not friends. I did not like him; he did not like me. I had never looked on him as quite human. It was amazing that a man so self-controlled, so urbane, accustomed to the usages of polite society, should break in upon a stranger with such a confession. I am naturally reticent. I should be ashamed, whatever I was suffering, to disclose my pain to another. I shivered. His weakness outraged me. For a moment I was filled with a passion of anger. How dared he thrust the anguish of his soul on me? I very nearly cried:

' "What the hell do I care?" '

Here the reader is put in possession of elements necessary to understanding Somerset Maugham as a writer: a very unusual sensibility instantly defended by an unamiable self-protective impulse, which in its turn is corrected by a more just response. In his handling of human beings, except in those instances where an entirely unpretentious sweetness of nature has disarmed him (Rosie, for example) these three reactions come into the play.

The 1914-18 war had a most important influence on the development of his talent: he was sent abroad as a Secret Service agent (see *Ashenden*). He learnt then how good it was for his talent to travel and to be alone. In the first place travel gave him new subjects. It is not right for a born story-teller to settle down. How much we lost when Kipling ceased to knock about the world and became a Sussex squire interested in history and fairies! The story-teller should sit loosely in the saddle of life; he need not rough it physically, but it is necessary for him to rough it spiritually. While it is almost irresistible to a successful novelist to settle down in comfortable surroundings of his own choosing, if he yields to that temptation he inevitably cuts himself off from sources of inspiration. It is essential, for the objective story-teller, at any rate, to come into contact with all sorts of human beings, and to adventure in worlds different from his own. It is to Mr Somerset Maugham's habit, after the First World War, of constant travel that we owe many of his striking stories, last, though not least, *The Narrow Corner*. But travel, besides supplying him with subjects, has enriched his work in other ways. Strange surroundings forced him to cultivate further his powers of description and invited him to record not only things seen but the emotion with which he saw them. His later books show an enormous advance in the art of handling words. The prose of such records of travel as *The Gentleman in the Parlour* is alive with a sensibility absent from the dry, able, drab notations of fact, in, say, *Of Human Bondage*. It has a rhythm that is not merely readable but moving. Readers of *The Narrow Corner*, too, will have recognised in its descriptions all the old sincerity but a new heed for beauty. Travel has helped him, too, I think, as an artist in a deeper way. It has soothed his loneliness by relieving the pressure of social life and its obligations, and also purified that detachment on which his power as an imaginative critic of life rests. It has widened not only his experience, but his attitude towards human nature. A larger tolerance, a more profound, and yet a more merciful indictment of humanity is perceptible in his later work. In 1921 I thought of him as a cynic. I wrote:

Cynicism is, of course, a vague term. What I mean by it here is scepticism with regard to the depth and persistence of human affection, disillusionment with the excitements of passion, the conviction that men and women are competitive, ostentatious and selfish, and only superficially sympathetic, that time in the end gets the better of even those who are most intelligently selfish, and a lack of faith in any cause of traditional morality. In the aquarium of life he sees aristocratic sharks, humble, greedy pike, gorgeous octopuses, fair, drifting jelly-fish, and occasionally he notices a flat, good-natured sole at the bottom of the tank who is content to lie modestly in the sand. It is a slight relief to contemplate such an uncompetitive creature, but the more permanent consolations come from the amusements of luxury and the security of wealth. If you ask me from where I have drawn the impression that this is really his 'world-view', I cannot point to any one play or novel. I feel it lurking behind his laughter, which is never really merry, his sense of values as they are exhibited in his character drawing, and, above all, behind the gaps in his picture of human relations.

And all this is still true enough of him, but it is no longer the whole truth. He might well have remained a cynic had he continued to study only the human specimens in the social aquarium. But if you read his later work receptively, *The Gentleman in the Parlour*, for example, which is among his books what *Sur l'eau* is in the works of Maupassant, sombre and beautiful, entertaining and sincere, you cannot miss a greatness of mind and sensitiveness to suffering common to both these masters of the art of story-telling.

W. H. DAVIES

1934

I HAD a curious experience some months ago. I was one of a small company who might, on the whole, be called distinguished; and one of them, a poet who certainly deserves the name, read out after dinner a composition by a young man in whose work he had faith. There was, at any rate, 'something there', he thought; whether it would unfold or not he could not tell. Gravely, beautifully he read the poem aloud—and not one of us understood one single line! We were clever; we were well-read; we were experts in catching suggestions, in seizing and dropping adroitly imaginative clues, and two of us at least had had practice in following intricate trains of reflection. Yet, at the conclusion, from the nature of the case, our comments could only be blurred expansions of the statement that there *might* be 'something there'. Mysterious criterion! If at any point in its progress that poem had conveyed some gleam of meaning, some trace of coherent sentiment, or even an image or two, we were an audience not unqualified (hard as it is to estimate a poem on first reading), to form a provisional opinion upon its value and genuineness, and on the literary skill with which the words had been arranged. But none of the tests which, up till today, have been applied to verse and prose since literature began were here of use. As the reader pointed out, with the exception of the suggestion of a hawk, no passage was even visual in its appeal: the poem was 'abstract' from beginning to end. The demand made upon the listener was that he should yield himself to a flow of words conveying neither images nor sentiments nor thoughts, in the faith that the whole would somehow wake in him an emotion that was truly 'poetical'. The postulate of such productions is that 'poetry' is an essence independent of what a poem says—probably best taken 'neat'. The same postulate underlies modern abstract painting.

Now, at no other period of the world's history would it have been possible to get people to listen with hopeful respect to a pitch-dark rigmarole. For me the most significant aspect of the evening was this light incidentally thrown upon the nature of our times. In art, I said to myself, surely the dead have votes. Then, what a tiny granule, sliver, driblet of a minority were those today who are attempting to deflect tradition.

Yet every generation (though each is but a jerk of the second-hand upon the clock of time) must explore new possibilities. Admitting that, what made it hard to attend to the new poetry and the new painting? On the face of it, the hedonist in me ought to have made me lean to that side, since to discover a fresh source of aesthetic pleasure is pure gain. Yet it is hedonism that I find pulling me the other way. The effect of the critical propaganda which accompanies the modern verse movement is to choke the springs of certain delight.

One of the prominent fuglemen of the modern movement has, I am told, declared in print that no poetry was written in England (with the exception perhaps of Donne's and a few scraps in other writers) between Shakespeare and Gerard Hopkins! What a desert (if he has been correctly reported) Mr Leavis's ardour leaves behind it! It seems to me a dubious bargain to lose a Keats to gain a Pound, to surrender a Coleridge to find a Flint, to exchange a Milton even for an Eliot. But must it be with us always either this poet or that? Does not the same reader often respond both to Pope and Blake? Surely we are all gifted with a happy natural inconsistency of taste? Indeed, we are—if only we let ourselves alone. We can admire poets equally who have hardly one excellence in common, until we apply to both the same Aesthetic. But the moment we start thinking we know what is the essence of poetry we are driven to reject much that we could otherwise admire. If Mr Leavis applied to the poetry of Shakespeare the tests he has presumably applied to that of the eighteenth and nineteenth centuries, Shakespeare would shrink to a very small compass indeed. Yes, there *is* a definite breach with tradition, though modern poets often deny it. Its symptom is a tolerance, not to say encouragement, of obscurity, which, though here and there passages in old poets can be quoted as precedents, is clean contrary to the spirit in which they wrote. It is the same, of course, with 'abstract' painting, which flaunts indifference to qualities old masters highly valued.

Now, there would be no need to become hot if this movement had not baleful consequences. But one source of its attraction is undoubtedly that within it the gifted and incompetent start under more equal conditions. In the poem not written to be understood, the difference between pretender and poet is not easy to perceive. Not only is it hard for others to find the former out, but, blessing of blessings, he cannot even find out himself! The other baleful consequence is that readers come to regard poetry as a mysterious product of words, unconnected with their valued emotions, except in so far as recognition of that mysterious result is accompanied by peculiar emotion. The root of my distrust of the modern movement is that by implication and example it dethrones poetry from the place it has held in the common life of man.

The above reflections, which have delayed me too long, were prompted by re-reading the poems of W. H. Davies. How, I asked myself, could eyes grown accustomed to the obscurity of the modern poem, how could minds habituated to the excitement (which, by the by, is not itself an aesthetic pleasure) of snatching at clues, and of combining, probably arbitrarily, shattered hints, respond to verse as simple and confiding as this? I recalled the current contempt for 'nature' poetry. Certainly rustic themes can inspire poor poetry, so, for the matter of that, can the copulation of crocodiles. Could readers bitten with the fascination of psychological darkness care for such a lyric as 'The King Fisher'?:

It was the Rainbow gave thee birth,
    And left thee all her lovely hues;
And, as her mother's name was Tears,
    So runs it in thy blood to choose
For haunts the lonely pools, and keep
In company with trees that weep.

Go you and, with such glorious hues,
    Live with proud peacocks in green parks;
On lawns as smooth as shining glass,
    Let every feather show its marks;
Get thee on boughs and clap thy wings
Before the windows of proud kings.

Nay, lovely bird, thou art not vain;
    Thou hast no proud ambitious mind;
I also love a quiet place
    That's green, away from all mankind;
A lonely pool, and let a tree
Sigh with her bosom over me.

Or such a 'conceit' as this?:

Nature has made my mind a mint,
    My thoughts are coins, on which I live;
The dies, with which I stamp my thoughts,
    Trees, blossoms, birds, and children give.

Sometimes my die's a homeless man,
    Or babes that have no milk and perish;
Sometimes it is a lady fair,
    Whose grace and loveliness I relish.

But all my love-thoughts, until now,
    Were false to utter, and must cease;
And not another coin must pass
    Without your image on each piece.

So, you shall be my queen from now,
    Your face on every thought I utter;
And I'll be rich—although the world
    May judge my metal's worth no better.

Or such a love lyric as this?:

> Tell them, when you are home again,
>   How warm the air was now;
> How silent were the birds and leaves,
>   And of the moon's full glow;
>   And how we saw afar
>   A falling star:
> It was a tear of pure delight
> Ran down the face of Heaven this happy night.
>
> Our kisses are but love in flower,
>   Until that greater time
> When, gathering strength, those flowers take wing,
>   And Love can reach his prime.
>   And now, my heart's delight,
>   Good night, good night;
> Give me the last sweet kiss—
> But do not breathe at home one word of this!

These, and many and many another poem he has written, derive from a sure tradition: the playful and tender genius of man's gratitude for beauty.

> What is this life if full of care,
> We have no time to stand and stare?
>
> No time to stand beneath the boughs
> And stare as long as sheep or cows.
>
> No time to see, when woods we pass,
> Where squirrels hide their nuts in grass.
>
> No time to see, in broad daylight,
> Streams full of stars, like skies at night.
>
> No time to turn at Beauty's glance,
> And watch her feet, how they can dance.
>
> No time to wait till her mouth can
> Enrich that smile her eyes began.
>
> A poor life this—if full of care,
> We have no time to stand and stare.

W. H. Davies has the most delightfully spontaneous lyrical
gift of any poet now writing. Perhaps we must go back to
Herrick to match that gift. Listen to this poem, 'A Great Time':

> Sweet Chance, that led my steps abroad,
>   Beyond the town, where wild flowers grow—
> A rainbow and a cuckoo, Lord,
>   How rich and great the times are now!
>   Know, all ye sheep
>   And cows, that keep
> On staring that I stand so long
>   In grass that's wet from heavy rain—
> A rainbow and a cuckoo's song
>   May never come together again;
>   May never come
>   This side the tomb.

I do not think he has written anything as classically perfect
as Herrick's best lyrics, as 'What needs complaints . . . ' or 'A
sweet disorder in the dress'. Nor are his rhythms quite so
subtle as in such a passage from Herrick as this:

> Alas! for me, that I have lost
>   E'en all almost;
> Sunk is my sight, set is my sun,
> And all the loom of life undone:
> The staff, the elm, the prop, the sheltering wall
>   Whereon my vine did crawl,
> Now, now blown down; needs must the old stock fall.

Although Herrick's *Hesperides* is full of hasty trifles, he
was not an extemporiser. Davies, in a poem called 'Bird and
Brook', speaks of his own poems, saying, 'My song that's bird-
like in its kind'; Herrick's song is never bird-like. Even in its
lightest capers, it resembles in virtuosity a performance on the
harpsichord. He has Horace's *curiosa felicitas*; Davies has
felicitas, but it is hardly *curiosa*. Impishness they have in
common, and that of Davies, as those who read *Hesperides*
through will discover, is of a far more amiable kind. Neither
of these born lyricists is passionate, but Herrick appears to have

more intellect because he was something of a classical scholar, and because he took more exacting pains. Davies will slip along the easy path even when he is writing his best; he will often, in a stanza of four lines, drop two rhymes which were needed for perfection.

Probably had he been more exacting towards himself (mastery of technique not being easy to him), he would have had to work too slowly, and many of his delightful things might have been lost in the effort to express them. 'He resembles Herrick', Mr R. C. Trevelyan once wrote, 'in possessing that rare power of creating in readers a mood of personal sympathy, and even of affection, so that, when he is not at his best, we are disposed to be tolerant and are always prepared whole-heartedly to enjoy his felicities, of which there are many.' That is what I, too, felt while reading his collected poems. And I knew I was drinking at the spring of certain delight.

KIPLING

1936

WHEN Kipling died my mind went back to 1898, when he was lying so gravely ill in New York that there seemed small chance of his recovery: to the public anxiety, and the bulletins, posted up two or three times a day, so urgent was the demand for news. 1898 marked the highest point of his popular renown in England and America. To English-speaking peoples, he then seemed to represent in literature deep instincts of their race. How young he was and yet how much he had achieved! But after the Boer War, Kipling never again stood in quite the same relation to his country; the heyday of British Imperialism was over, and the national spirit was too divided to find complete expression in his work, though he remained the mouthpiece of a very large section of the public. Those were the days when a Frenchman could actually write a book called *A quoi tient la supériorité des Anglo-Saxons?* and the Continent was searching Kipling's works for the answer. But all this is unimportant today to those who are endeavouring to make up their minds about Kipling's permanent *place* among English writers.

Let us run over what are the most obvious things to say about him; they are not all of them of the first importance, but together they make an imposing impression. He was a genius, there's no doubt about that. He was a most conscientious and able craftsman. He stood for a number of years in a symbolic relation to the spirit of his times. He was recognised as a master of the short story and he was *the bard* of the British Empire. I don't propose to say anything about him as the poet of Imperialism, but to recall certain of his characteristics as a craftsman, as a writer, as a teller of tales.

First, however, one other thing must be said. However much

opinions may differ about his work, Rudyard Kipling has been
the most wide-flung combustion in the sky of English letters
since Byron and Dickens. This, no doubt, was partly due, as
it was with Byron, to the representative and political character
of his work, but it was by no means due entirely to that. Let's
consider for a moment other causes of the astonishing width of
his appeal. Although his style possessed one of the most
important qualifications for immense popularity, namely, un-
flagging vigour, it displayed at the same time an unpopular
quality: extreme virtuosity. In his later work especially his
prose was marked by an acrobatic verbal ingenuity hardly
exceeded by Meredith. It seems on the face of it strange that
an author who is so tremendously concentrated and latterly
elliptical should have continued to appeal to *non-literary*
readers. Kipling is a writer whose phrases must be allowed to
soak a moment in the mind before they expand, like those little
Japanese pellets which blossom into flower only when they have
lain awhile on the surface of a cup of water. Yet with all his
ostentatious word-craft, he remained a favourite author of
thousands upon thousands of readers who are ordinarily impatient of that kind of writing. No author, too, had a more
various audience of admirers, while, oddly enough, it was
among *literary* people, among literary artists and critics, that
this master craftsman was apt to meet with grudging appreciation. We admitted his genius, his power, but we often wrote
and talked as though we were sorry we had to.

What then were the qualities which made him admired by
millions and yet often abused by those who loved, as he did,
the painful art of writing? Of course, many of those who
criticised him coolly or adversely were those who also hated his
politics and his morals. These pervade his work. They are as
tribal as a Prussian historian's, or a schoolboy's. Even when
addressing children, the savour of them was pervasive, and
because it was Kipling who was writing, their savour was
invariably pungent. That important fact, however, is not the
most interesting one. His style, while loved by the unliterary,

often irritated the literary because the aim of his virtuosity was always a *violent precision*. His adjectives and phrases start from the page. He forced you first and foremost to see, to hear, to touch and to smell—above all to see and smell as vividly as words can be made to compass those ends. In Kipling, when the greatest vividness was inconsistent with an aesthetic impression—well, that kind of beauty went by the board. His metaphors and comparisons are apt to be chosen (and like all vivid writers he used them continually) with complete indifference to associations and overtones, and with a single aim—vividness. To take an example from his *Letters of Travel*: 'There was never a cloud in the sky, that rested upon the snowline of the horizon as a sapphire on white velvet.' Now we have all seen a sapphire on white velvet in a jeweller's window, and it calls up vividly the intense blue of dark sky above a snowfield, but that comparison does not bring out, it even destroys the beauty of the picture itself. Of course, this is not true of all his comparisons and metaphors. Some had poetry and depth. What fine phrases and sentences he found to describe the sea in *Captains Courageous*; for instance, the sleek swell before storms, 'grey, formless, enormous and growing', or 'the heave and the halt and the howl and the crash of the comber windhounded'. Think, too, of the scenes that rose before our minds while reading *Kim*! No writer triumphed more completely in combining the arresting detail and wide horizons (so hard to do) into one picture. But this trend of his style towards perpetual vividness, to which beauty was often sacrificed, alienated the more aesthetic type of reader. None of his contemporaries could condense more into a brief description. I cannot resist giving one more example. Here is the opening of one of his later stories about a break-down of a motor on the Great North Road. The story resolves itself into a fantastic discourse by an American on the ruinous effects of Prohibition—a linguistic feast, but empty of lasting interest. Listen:

By the time we had found the trouble, night shut down on us. A rounded pile of woods ahead took one sudden star to its forehead and faded out; the way-waste melted into the darker velvet of the hedge, another star reflected itself in the glassy black of the bitumened road; and a weak moon struggled up out of a mist-patch from a valley. *Our lights painted the grass unearthly greens, and the tree-boles bone-white.* A church clock struck eleven, as I curled up in the front seat and waited the progress of Time and Things, with some notion of picking up a tow towards morning.

But now let's turn to the *other* sources of his immense popularity. Everyone likes a good story, and Kipling was an admirable story-teller. But it was not only that. The short story-teller is more dependent than any other kind of literary artist upon lucky choice in his subject. If one looks through the works of the world's famous short-story writers—Maupassant, Chekhov, Henry James, Kipling himself, Ambrose Bierce, and today Mr Somerset Maugham—one sees that it is only when the writer has hit upon a story *good in itself* that he has written memorably. His other stories, though they may be as skilfully told and presented, do not make a deep impression. In the short-story the theme is all important. It is only from time to time in an author's career that a good theme comes to hand. Master as Kipling was of description, of recording distinctive speech (a gift so necessary where there is no space to expound character), his fine stories might all be comprised in a single volume. It was not only his skill in description, not even his power of heightening characteristics by intensifying modes of speech (we all remember his soldiers' talk and that of the enormous variety of men and women who figure in his pages), but an interest more fundamental which took the world by storm. He made every character in his stories an artist in his own lingo: the schoolboy, the engineer, the soldier, the bagman —even, by a stretch of the imagination, different kinds of animals, in the *Jungle Books*. But the most significant thing of all about him as a story-teller was that he put these gifts at the service *not* of the love-story, not of some adventure in sensibility, not of worldly success, but for the first time at the service of a man's *relation to his work*, whether that work was departmental, military, journalistic; whether it was medical, building a bridge, running an engine or stopping a famine or commanding a ship; whether it was a common job or a unique one.

Instantly, all over the world the sympathy of all sorts and conditions of readers went out to hug an author whose theme was a man's relation to his work; how a man could stick to it even when sickened by it, see it through in spite of defeat, loneliness and weakness. This is a more pervasive characteristic of Kipling's work than what sometimes seemed most prominent— its connection with militarism and Empire building. He idealised for an enormous variety of men their relation to their work: and such stories were a 'felt want', as they say in the advertising world, they satisfied a stronger thirst than that for exotic colour and adventure, though Kipling also provided that.

Connected with this sense of a man's relation to his job was his strong sense of group loyalty—the herd instinct, whether it took the form of patriotism, or schoolhouse against school, or school against the world, or regiment against War Office. The romance and meaning of life lay according to Kipling in the bee's devotion to the hive. Kipling was the poet of the herd instinct, and to such a writer independence of thought presents itself as the most insidious enemy. The diameter of his mind was not wide. He distrusted 'thought', knowing that it separates men, or rather unites them only on a plane of which he had little cognisance and seen from which group emotions and group morale appear narrow. Hence the permanent quarrel between him and the thinking sort, whether they were artists themselves, or people preoccupied with things of the mind. Put yourself in the heart and mind of a young aesthetic intellectual at the beginning of the century and you will feel Kipling to be your *enemy*, an honourable and strong enemy; but an enemy, and thank goodness an enemy who was *afraid* of *you* —or rather of thought. I say independence of thought was Kipling's enemy, not independence of action. In nothing was he more representative of the Anglo-Saxon character, American as well as English, than in his admiration, his demand, for individual responsibility in decision. M. André Chevrillon, his brilliant translator, has analysed well this combination in Kipling's work between emotional herd-loyalty and the necessity of being able to act on personal initiative. This conception of duty as something ultimately *self*-imposed, not commanded from without, is the moral soul of Protestantism. And it is the final test Rudyard Kipling applied to men.

In later years he treated new subjects. His style lost some of its early violent vitality and became more elaborate. But the main difference between his earlier and his later phase was that latterly he used his gifts for vivid presentation more often upon things dreamt through than lived through. His extraordinary avidity of attention to the actual lost something of its bite. *Puck of Pook's Hill, Rewards and Fairies* were inspired by his love of a *past* England. On the other hand, to sit loosely in the saddle of life, to roam, rough it, listen to travellers' yarns and to the talk of workers in all parts of the earth, had been more likely to bring him the short story-teller's lucky finds. As a Sussex squire he continued to travel, but chiefly in the past; his creative work was fed henceforth mostly by books and dreams.

Was Kipling a great poet? He was not a minor poet, that is certain—as certain as that Byron was not a minor poet. But when I ask myself that question, I cannot remember anything of his to put beside the finest poetry. Nevertheless he lifted into the middle realm of poetry more moods and enthusiasms characteristic of active men than any of his contemporaries; and not one poet among them made so spirited, so sincere, so unselfconscious an attempt to handle in verse the romance of modern invention, or to celebrate the new opportunities for adventure and sensation opened up by modern life. He wrote poems about what a farmer felt watching his fat cattle go through a gate, what an ex-soldier thought while mowing the vicar's lawn, what an engineer felt about his engine. He wrote poems not only about love and death—the eternal themes—but what the average man felt to be romantic in his daily life.

There is a feeling abroad that it is time the Muse ceased to repeat her ancient divinations and that she dealt with *everyday* emotions, with *common* not *rare*, experiences. Who else has made, anything like so spirited, so sincere, so unselfconscious an effort to do so?

LESLIE STEPHEN

1937

JUDGED by their influence upon men's minds alone, the writings which Leslie Stephen collected in *Essays on Free-thinking and Plain-speaking* (1873), and in *An Agnostic's Apology* (1893) (most of the latter written much earlier), must be considered the most important part of his life's work. One reason, as we shall be presently reminded, why he wrote disparagingly of literary criticism was that it seemed so trivial compared with criticism of thought and religion. What if he *had* induced some readers to take a clearer view of the merits and limitations of Fielding or De Quincey, or if he *had* succeeded in giving a tolerably true account of some man's life? Of what importance was that compared with helping men to a truer conception of the nature of things, or with the work of a man of science? This reflection, which often visited him, robbed him of retrospective satisfaction in his books, though while writing them he derived keen pleasure from knocking nails on the head. He knew that his controversial writings had made an impression on the public, who think by fits and starts, but before the end of the nineteenth century his controversial work was over. He could have only repeated himself. What else of value outside controversy had Leslie Stephen achieved?

I will try to answer that question which he often put despondently to himself; to describe the kind of criticism he wrote, and, using also external evidence, the man who was behind it. This was his own way of setting about criticism; indeed, the most comprehensive description of Leslie Stephen as a critic would be to call him an expert in character, if that is also taken as implying connoisseurship in defining points of view. It is his conception of the writer that gives unity to most of his literary essays; not the relation of a book to the history of literature or to some standard of perfection. What he investigated with greater interest was the relation of a book to its author. Of course, this did not preclude his pointing out with great acuteness, as he went along, an author's successes or failures as a craftsman, or reminding us of the pertinence or the folly of a work as a commentary on life; but as a critic he directed our attention chiefly to the sort of man the author had apparently been; to the man who saw and felt things thus and thus, and expressed himself in this way and no other.

The title of his last four volumes of criticism, *Studies of a Biographer*, is in no small degree applicable to his first collection of critical essays, *Hours in a Library*. In his essay on 'Shakespeare the Man', we find him writing:

> Now I confess that to me one main interest in reading is always the communion with the author. *Paradise Lost* gives me the sense of intercourse with Milton, and the *Waverley Novels* bring me a greeting from Scott. Every author, I fancy, is unconsciously his own Boswell, and, however 'objective' or dramatic he professes to be, really betrays his own secrets. . . . Self-revelation is not the less clear because involuntary or quite incidental to the main purpose of a book. I may read Gibbon simply to learn facts; but I enjoy his literary merits because I recognise my friend of the autobiography who 'sighed as a lover and obeyed as a son'. I may study Darwin's *Origin of Species* to clear my views upon natural selection; but as a book it interests me even through the defects of style by the occult personal charm of the candid, sagacious, patient seeker for truth. In pure literature the case is, of course, plainer, and I will not count up instances because, in truth, I can hardly think of a clear exception. Whenever we know a man adequately we perceive that, though different aspects of his character may be made prominent in his life and his works, the same qualities are revealed in both, and we cannot describe the literary without indicating the personal charm.

Now a critic who approaches his subjects in this spirit will inevitably discourse more about human nature and morals than about art, and Leslie Stephen is the least aesthetic of noteworthy critics. In this connection his strenuous evangelical upbringing must not be overlooked; through both his father and his mother his home was affiliated to the Clapham Sect.

He is constantly harping on 'sincerity'. Sincerity is a condition of all satisfactory personal relations, and therefore a condition of the communion between writer and reader which he valued most. In his essay on Sterne, whom he finds deficient in that respect, he says:

> The qualification must, of course, be understood that a great book really expresses the most refined essence of the writer's character. It gives the author transfigured and does not represent all the stains and distortions which he may have received in his progress through the world.
> If this be true in some degree of all imaginative writers, it is especially true of humorists. For humour is essentially the expression of a personal idiosyncrasy. . . . We love the humour in short so far as we love the character from which it flows.

He could not bring himself to love Sterne, which I (though love may be too strong a word) find no difficulty in doing. He examined his life, especially his married life and his flirtations, with severity, and he concluded that 'Sterne was a man who understood to perfection the art of enjoying his own good feelings as a luxury without humbling himself to translate them into practice' (Stephen's definition of a sentimentalist). The judgment pronounced by Thackeray on Sterne seemed to him substantially unimpeachable. He strongly reprobated Sterne's trick of inclining our thoughts (before we realise it) gently towards indecency. With that sense of fun which delights to trip up the dignity of the reader, trusting to his smiling afterwards, he had no sympathy.

Nevertheless, it must not be supposed that this essay, perhaps more likely than any other in *Hours in a Library* to strike our contemporaries as missing the point, is without warmly appreciative passages. Referring to Sterne's touches of exquisite precision, he says that 'they give the impression that the thing has been done once for all'. Two or three of the scenes in which Uncle Toby expresses his sentiments struck him as being 'as perfect in their way as the half-dozen lines in which Mrs Quickly describes the end of Falstaff; and Uncle Toby's

oath', he declares to be 'a triumph fully worthy of Shakespeare';
but, he adds, 'the recording angel, though he comes in effectively,
is a little suspicious to me'. While admitting the felicity with
which the scene is presented, he suggests that it would have
been really stronger had the angel been omitted (by stronger,
he means more moving), 'for the angel seems to introduce an
unpleasant air as of eighteenth-century politeness; we fancy that
he would have welcomed a Lord Chesterfield to the celestial
mansions with a faultless bow and a dexterous compliment'.

Perfectly true. But to wish on that account the angel away
is surely to miss the point of Sterne, whose attitude towards all
emotions was playful. No doubt Sterne thought that here, or
in the bravura passage on the dead donkey, he was achieving
the acme of pathos. But his temperament was stronger than
any conscious intention; consequently what in effect we enjoy,
as everywhere in Sterne, is an elegant ambiguity. As with some
other Irishmen known to fame, Sterne's heart was in his
imagination. The infection we catch from him is, as Goethe
noticed, a light fantastic sense of freedom; a state of mind
(Shandyism) in which we enjoy together the pleasures of
extravagant sensibility, and a feeling that nothing much matters.

Leslie Stephen's attitude towards Sterne's pathetic passages
was the same as Dr Johnson's, who, when Miss Monckton said:
'I am sure they have affected me', replied smiling and rolling
himself about, 'That is because, dearest, you are a dunce.'
Johnson set no store by airy detachment, nor could he believe
that posterity would cherish its products. Did he not point to
Sterne as an instance of the ephemeral nature of all reputations
founded on the fantastic? Leslie Stephen had no sense of the
fantastic, or of the charm of the artificial; it is one of the dumb
notes on his piano. He wanted to be moved; and more—he
wanted to be certain that the author had been moved himself.

'We are always pursued in reading Pope', he says, 'by dis-
agreeable misgivings. We don't know what comes from the
heart, and what from the lips. As a banker's clerk can tell a
bad coin by its ring on the counter, without need of a testing

apparatus, the true critic can instinctively estimate the amount
of bullion in Pope's epigrammatic tinsel. But criticism of this
kind, as Pope truly says, is as rare as poetical genius. Humbler
writers must be content to take their weights and measures, or,
in other words, to test their first impression, by such external
evidence as is available.'

Leslie Stephen did not trust himself to tell good coin by its
ring, or perhaps it would be truer to say he thought he ought
not to. Certainly, investigations into the genuineness of an
author require a testing apparatus, even when conducted by
a critic of rapid intuitions. In the case of Pope that investi-
gation ended unfavourably.

Johnson was the man after Leslie Stephen's heart. Of his
five biographical monographs in the *English Men of Letters*, his
Johnson is the best, and it is equal to the very best in that
excellent series. Johnson was the man he loved most in
literature, though not (need it be said?) the writer he admired
most, which incidentally throws some doubt on his critical
method. Johnson as a writer seemed to him 'a great force half
wasted because the fashionable costume of the day hampered
the free exercise of his powers'; but Johnson as he is known
through the records of his life and his talk embodied nearly
all the qualities which Leslie Stephen admired most in other
writers.

We cannot be in Johnson's company long without becoming
aware that what attracts us to him so strongly is that he combined a disillusioned estimate of human nature, sufficient to
launch twenty little cynics, with a craving for love and sympathy so urgent that it would have turned a weaker nature into
a benign sentimentalist, and in a lesser degree this is what
attracts us in Leslie Stephen. His raciest passages might often
be described as cynical. There are also evidences of deep
feeling. There is a Johnsonian contempt for those who look
only upon the bright side of life or human nature, equalled only
by a contempt for those who adopt a querulous or dainty tone.

Leslie Stephen was born in 1832, not 1709, which implies

considerable differences, and allowing for those, it is tempting to describe his critical work as an attempt to go on writing, in the nineteenth century, Johnson's *Lives of the Poets*. He was more at home with prose writers; but the poets he did study were Pope, Crabbe, Coleridge, Wordsworth, Tennyson and Matthew Arnold; Shelley in so far as his poetry is related to the ideas of Godwin; Cowper in so far as he could be compared with Rousseau, and Donne—but only in relation to his times. The essays on Tennyson and Matthew Arnold contain little literary criticism. The former gives an account of what Tennyson's poetry meant to Stephen's generation, and shows a strong preference for the earlier poetry. In the essay on Arnold he expresses the same impatience at being told again and again, however melodiously, that the wisest of us must take dejectedly 'his seat upon the intellectual throne', keeping as our only friend 'sad patience, too near neighbour to despair'.

It is impossible to imagine a Matthew Arnold who had never been at Oxford and a Leslie Stephen who had never been at Cambridge. The stamp which this University left on him was lasting. The fourteen years he spent there as an undergraduate and a fellow of Trinity Hall, from 1850 to 1864, decided what he was to admire and trust in men and books throughout his life. A famous definition might be modified to fit him: Criticism is the adventures of the soul of Cambridge among masterpieces. Souls like bodies change. Perhaps that of Cambridge has changed or is changing; from time to time indications of that possibility have lately reached me. All I can say is that the spirit of Cambridge in the late 'nineties was very like indeed to that which Leslie Stephen knew and carried away with him. He was well aware that some of these adventures might cause outsiders to blaspheme, and there is a recurring note in his criticism—I will not call it apologetic, it was often humorously defiant—which amounts now and then to an admission that possibly the soul of Cambridge had no business at all to embark on such adventures; to risk perdition in regions where reason is at a disadvantage compared with intuition, and the habits are encouraged of skimming over intellectual difficulties, and deviating into the delicate impertinences of egotism. As a practising critic he limited himself as far as he could to that aspect of his subject about which it was possible to argue. He was a man of letters who would have preferred to be a philosopher or a man of science. His moving essay on Wordsworth was, as its title 'Wordsworth's Ethics' suggests, chiefly a commentary on the poet's thought and the value of his poetry to those in sorrow.

'Other poetry becomes trifling when we are making our inevitable passage through the Valley of the Shadow of Death. Wordsworth's alone retains its power.' The essay was written shortly after the death of his first wife, Thackeray's daughter, in 'seventy-five.

The provinces of the poet and philosopher were in his view concentric but not coincident, and the poetry he felt best able to criticise was that kind which could be most directly reconverted from the expression of emotion into thought. But he was well aware that this was not all that was required of a critic of poetry. He was well aware of the danger, though he did not always avoid it, of applying strong sense to inappropriate topics, and falling into the error of Johnson in his criticism of *Lycidas* and Gray.

His first impulses of admiration he seldom felt able to analyse, and nothing would induce him merely to 'shriek and clasp his hands in ecstasy'. And yet from childhood he had been particularly susceptible to poetry, and few men have been able to repeat more of it by heart. He was one of the fortunates who do not need to learn verse that has delighted them; and it was a persistent habit of his to rumble it out on his solitary walks, which in one of his gaunt, abstruse appearance was apt to startle passers-by. As a child, poetry and such books as the *Arabian Nights* had often excited him to a degree alarming to his parents; and since he was both nervously shy and deplorably feeble in physique, his early education was deliberately planned to correct an extreme sensibility. It was while at

Cambridge that he changed physically and temperamentally, first into an enthusiastic oar, then into a rowing-coach famous for his wind on the towing path, and incidentally into one of the first Alpine climbers and long-distance walkers of his day. In mind he became an almost fanatical admirer of intellect, and a mathematician. He also became a clergyman, but for several years he was so entirely absorbed in his life as a fellow and tutor of Trinity Hall that he did not realise the falseness of his position.

'I had taken orders', he wrote in *Some Early Impressions*, 'rashly, though not, I trust, with conscious insincerity, on a sort of tacit understanding that Maurice or his like would act as an interpreter of the true facts. . . . It may be easy to read any meaning into a dogma, but since allegorising has gone out of fashion, historical narratives are not so malleable. They were, it seemed to me, true or false, and could not be both at once. Divines, since that day, have discovered that it is possible to give up the history without dropping a belief in revelation. I could not then, as I cannot now, take that view. I had to give up my profession. . . . In truth, I did not feel that the solid ground was giving way beneath my feet, but rather that I was being relieved of a cumbrous burden. I was not discovering that my creed was false, but that I had never really believed it.'

That confession is significant. His faith, while he possessed it, had not been accompanied by what is called spiritual life. He had never associated religion with his most valued emotions towards nature or man. The points at which he had touched Christianity had been purely moral, and these he took over intact into his new life: they were a contempt, not to say dread, of self-indulgence, a belief in the importance of chastity, and something approaching adoration for tenderness of heart, while his reprobation of the softer vices remained adamant.

In 1862, refusing to take services in Chapel, he resigned his tutorship and in 1867 his fellowship. Then he began to earn a living in London as a journalist. He had lingered on at Cambridge those last two years because the atmosphere of the place was singularly sympathetic to him. 'The one thing', he says, 'that can spoil the social intercourse of well-educated men living in great freedom from unnecessary etiquette is a spirit of misplaced zeal'; and from that Cambridge was blessedly free. There were also no prophets; prophets, though not necessarily humbugs in themselves, were apt, he thought, to be the cause of humbug in others. What he valued most at Cambridge were the friendships which spring from discussion; in the pursuit of truth he allowed the soul full play.

Perhaps this is the place to say something about his intellectual ambitions. Their nature as well as the direction of them had an effect on his criticism. Apparently he was not ambitious, but he was only not ambitious because, in literature at any rate, he thought only the highest achievement worth while; and that was out of his reach. One friend attributed to him the opinion that on the whole books ought *not* to be written; and there is occasionally something in the tone of his comments on authors which lends plausibility to that exaggeration. He would have gladly extended the condemnation of mediocre poetry ('In poetry there is no golden mean; mediocrity there is of a different metal') to every branch of literature. Yet he lived in a period of hero-worship, and was himself extremely susceptible to emotions of enthusiasm and reverence. His horror of gush was partly due to fear of failing to do justice to those almost sacred feelings. He held (and this was one of his first principles as a critic) that 'a man's weakness can rarely be overlooked without underestimating his strength'. Some of his studies in human nature might seem grudging, owing to the number of reservations they contain, until the reader has grasped that praise from Leslie Stephen, which he always strove to make precise, meant a very great deal.

His essays are an effective protest against the contemporary habit of debasing the currency of praise. He was absurdly humble about his own writings, partly, as I have said, because he would have far rather been a philosopher or a man of science, partly on account of this sense of the width of the gap between work of the first order and the next. It is possible that a tendency to dwell on that gap was self-consolatory; if he could be by no means reckoned among writers of the first order, others of no mean merit were likewise excluded. But only a constitutional diffidence, or, as he sometimes was inclined to suspect, an inverted conceit, can account for his humility in some directions. He even compared his own writing, with a sigh of inferiority, to that of John Morley, whose style, though it may have the appearance at a distance of marble, in texture resembles blancmange. At any rate you cannot poke holes in Leslie Stephen's page with an umbrella. There is no doubt he was a self-disappointed man. His editorship of the *Cornhill Magazine* gave him leisure to try his hand intermittently at solving the old Utilitarian problem of reconciling 'the general Happiness' with the principle of a rational egotism, and at proving that the 'good' had a survival value for society, though not necessarily for the individual. Many years afterwards, his daughter, Virginia Woolf, asked him which was his favourite among his books; all he would reply was that he knew which one he would like the world to think his best—*The Science of Ethics*. The reception of it disappointed him. Sidgwick, reviewing it in *Mind*, showed that he did not think the book had solved any of the difficulties he had raised himself in *The Methods of Ethics*. No second edition was ever called for. It was a work which had occupied Stephen off and on for six years. It was published in 1882, and, as the *Cornhill* was flagging at that time, his disappointment made him accept the editorship of *The Dictionary of National Biography*. He did not embark on this incalculably beneficent task with much enthusiasm. He describes it as 'a very laborious and, what was worse, a very worrying piece of work', and at the start the work was unfamiliar to him. He was not a researcher by inclination and he had not estimated the burden involved. 'I thought I should have time for other things and hoped the *Dictionary* would either die at once or make such a success that I might be able to content myself with superintending it and have a second-in-command.' He had a dangerous collapse in 1888. Volume XXII of the *Dictionary* was published in 1890 with the name of Sidney Lee, who had been his sub-editor from the start, also on the title page. This joint editorship continued till the twenty-seventh volume when, after an attack of influenza, Leslie Stephen resigned. How did he regard an achievement which has proved as important to our culture, as any recent scientific discovery to our comfort? He admits he 'came to take a certain pride in it'; but it evidently did not relieve that sense of failure which haunted him. After the death of his second wife, Mrs Duckworth, while he could think of nothing but the past, he wrote a long confidential letter to his children. In substance this document is an account of the two women he had loved, but it contains passages about himself:

I know, of course, that I am a man of ability—literary at any rate. I feel myself to be really in this superior to many more popular writers. I have received many high compliments from good judges. When I think (as my Julia used to tell me I might think) of the way in which my friends spoke of me, of Lowell and Norton and Croom Robertson and Sidgwick and Morley and G. Meredith and Morison and many others, I feel ungrateful in making my complaints: I am not a failure pure and simple: I am, I hold, a failure in this way: I have scattered myself over too many subjects. I think that I had it in me to write something which should make a real mark in ethical and philosophical speculation. Unluckily, what with journalism and the *Dictionary*, I have been too much of a Jack-of-all-trades, and instead of striking home in any one direction, have shown (as my friends admitted) capacity for striking. I don't think that this matters very much, as you shall see, but I do feel that if the history of English thought in this century should ever be written, my name will come in a footnote and small type, whereas, if my energies had been better directed, it might have occupied a paragraph, even a section of a chapter, in full-sized type. The cause is that want of self-confidence which I indicated as an early failing.

Had I fully succeeded and surpassed all my contemporaries in my own line, what should I have done? I should have written a book or two which might be read by my contemporaries and perhaps by the next generation, and which would have survived so long because they expressed a little better than others thoughts which were more or less common to thousands of people, many of them often a little less able than myself. Now I say, advisedly, that I do not think such an achievement as valuable as hers [his wife's].

This is not the place in which to repeat the tribute of his love and bereavement; but you will find a discussion of the relative values of private virtues and intellectual achievement or public services in Leslie Stephen's last lecture on 'Forgotten Bene-factors' in *Social Rights and Duties*.

In the core of his emotional nature he gave preference to the private virtues. It is sometimes even disconcerting to find how much this influenced him in deciding the value of an author's works to the world. He is, as might have been anticipated, severe towards Rousseau; and in so far as he relents, it is due to his discovering in Rousseau 'a redeeming quality', namely the value he set on the simple affections, on 'an idyllic life of calm domestic tranquillity', perhaps not unlike Cowper's delight in taking tea with Mrs Unwin, though streaked (oddly as it appears to Stephen) with 'a kind of sensual appetite for pure simple pleasures'. In Hazlitt he cannot stomach the *Liber Amoris*; in Coleridge, his having left Southey to look after Mrs Coleridge and the children; and in De Quincey he cannot overlook that the source of the awe-struck sense of the vast and vague, which De Quincey communicated so magnificently, was opium. In Thackeray, one of his favourite novelists, he sees no faults that seriously matter, since 'his writings mean, if they mean anything, that the love of a wife and child and friends is the one sacred element in our nature, of infinitely higher price than anything which can come into competition with it; and that Vanity Fair is what it is because it stimulates the pursuit of objects frivolous and unsatisfying just so far that they imply indifference to those emotions'. He is also lenient to Kingsley, partly because he detects in Kingsley the belief that 'the root of all that is good in man lies in the purity and vigour of the domestic affections'. In short, there are times when we are left wondering if a critic, in whom the exercise of the intellect was a passion, is not saying in effect: 'Be good, sweet maid,

and let who will be clever.' There are passages scattered
through his books which indicate that, compared with qualities
of heart, all others seemed to him like a row of figures preceded
by a decimal point and incapable of rising to the value of a
single unit.

That he underrated the value of his own work there is
no doubt. Even his masterly *English Thought in the Eighteenth
Century* failed to satisfy him. He knew it was well done,
but he doubted its value, since thought and imaginative
literature were only by-products of social evolution, 'the noise
that the wheels make as they go round', and therefore no history
of thought could be complete by itself. It was because Sainte-
Beuve had taken such pains to place every author in his social
setting and his times that he respected Sainte-Beuve's work so
much. The view held in France by some critics, and advocated
in England by Oscar Wilde and Walter Pater, that criticism
was the quintessence of literature appeared to him too absurd
to discuss. All the critic could do for his fellow-men was to
stimulate their interest in literature by pointing out what he
had himself enjoyed or not enjoyed, and by giving names to
the qualities he perceived in them. He could appeal to the
reader and say: Are not these, when you come to think it over,
the strong points of this book, and these the weak ones?

Stephen himself was deficient in the power of transmitting
the emotions he had derived himself from literature; he seldom,
if ever, attempted to record a thrill. But he excelled in describing the qualities of authors, whether he summed up for or
against them; and this is a most important part of the critic's
function. By focusing in a phrase our scattered impressions,
the critic confers an intellectual benefit which increases our
interest when we think over an author's works. True, we can
enjoy Defoe without noticing that his method of producing an
impression of reality is the same as that of the circumstantial
liar, who introduces details so fortuitous that it is hard to
believe he could have invented them; but when Leslie Stephen
says this, it brings suddenly together in our minds a number

of instances. And the same effect is produced by his remark that knowledge of human nature in Fielding is based on observation rather than intuitive sympathy. Leslie Stephen's critical essays are crammed with illuminating comments of this kind. Of course, they do not help us to decide whether the fiction in question is good or bad, any more than a naturalist's description of a beast necessarily throws light on its value to man. But criticism must be in great part a Natural History of Authors, in which are set forth their distinctive features, their adaptation to their environment, and their relations to other species. When it comes to judgment, the test which Leslie Stephen applied was the relation of a work to life, the extent to which it ministered, in one way or another, to all human good.

MAUPASSANT

1938

I

MAUPASSANT is among the French writers whose work I know best. (In England this is not uncommon.) It shows, however, an ill-proportioned knowledge of French literature. There are many greater French authors with whom intimate acquaintance would be far more rewarding. But there it is! I began to learn French by reading his short stories. They were also the first examples of 'daring' fiction I had come across; also the first stories in which I became aware how an apparent detachment on the author's part can heighten in transmission the emotions of pity, contempt, and despair. They brought me, too, the satisfaction so keen in youth of looking hard and straight at the worst sides of human nature. And then, I was born a lover of stories. Not of those fluffy, factless affairs, ending, perhaps, after nothing whatever has occurred, on this sort of note: 'Hypatia was glad she had lighted a fire. . . . Presently she walked over to the bird-cage and pushed a lump of sugar between the two already-widened bars of it. There she stood, making caressing sounds with her pursed lips. . . . Outside the window a chilly snow-dust was already sprinkling the almond-tree in blossom.' Very sad and significant, no doubt.

No, no, I do not care for that sort of short story; and to me it is a matter of wonder that any respectable reader can. The kind I like is that which cavemen probably enjoyed and repeated to each other; that the Greeks invented about gods and heroes; that medieval *jongleurs* earned a living by reciting, and Chaucer and Boccaccio wrote so well. The kind which, beside camp-fires, inn-fires, in railway trains, in nurseries, on walks, on board ships, in every sort of circumstance, at moments of expansion, depression, gaiety, perplexity, boredom, men have told each other since speech began. Good ones are not easy to find; and it is nearly always a matter of ringing the changes on old situations, with the addition of the flavour and those details which the personality of the narrator and his times supply.

Maupassant was a master of the anecdote. What brevity is to wit, concision is to the art of story-telling. The manner of telling it may seem leisurely, and gain a grace thereby, as it does in two charming stories by George Moore, 'A Letter to Rome' (*The Untilled Field*), and 'Wilfred' (*Celibate Lives*), or as it does in that masterpiece of Scott's, 'The Two Drovers'. But really, when any story is first-rate, the current is always running quite rapidly and never stagnates into pools.

Among our famous contemporaries Somerset Maugham has written a few beauties ('Alien Corn,' for example), and so, of course, has Kipling. But only a few. So important is it in this art to get hold of a good tale. Literary skill may disguise, but can never supply, the lack of that. Thus, it sometimes happens that an inferior writer achieves a good short story. (I have never forgotten one by Jerome K. Jerome about a Swiss guide who lost his bride in a crevasse, and I like one I have written myself.) The finding of a *story* is often a matter of luck. Psychological imagination, the gift of tracing the thoughts and changes of emotion in characters may even be a hindrance to the perfect telling of a short story. Only the craftfulness of Henry James could surmount the disabilities for this purpose inseparable from his supreme gift. His best short stories were either entirely subjective, like 'The Altar of the Dead'; or they dealt with the predicaments of the artist ('The Lesson of the Master', 'The Velvet Glove', 'The Middle Years'); or they were those (wider in appeal) in which he employed his curiously fine apprehension of a *possible* supernatural, and approached, so characteristically, our susceptibility to terror through the moral sense: 'The Turn of the Screw', 'The Jolly Corner'.

But literary virtuosity also may be a drawback to the story-teller. Thus, Flaubert's *Trois Contes* (I do not except even

'Un Cœur Simple' in that volume) suffers from an excess of elaboration. Kipling, too, especially in his later stories, yielded too much to the temptation to strike a spark out of everything. A knotted terseness often interrupts the flow of narrative; attention is continually arrested, whether in admiration or pain, when it should be gliding with the stream. The norm of the art of the anecdote is, after all, that the style of it should just conceivably be that of *viva voce* narration. There are, of course, endless opportunities left for virtuosity in precision of statement and description within that manner. The stories in Max Beerbohm's *Seven Men* are masterly in this respect; while the most delicate adjustment in them of lightness of tone to slightness of theme, makes it possible to enjoy them again and again. They pass *the* test: few stories read aloud so smoothly and well. Whoever reads them to others seems the while to enjoy himself the pleasures of authorship. I have never done so without feeling a glow of pride.

Now the style of Maupassant is not loquitive, but its rhythms are so easy and undulatory, its transitions so natural and its tone so personal and uniform that the reader readily accepts it as a narrator's medium. It can rise in reflection and description to a sonority not unworthy of his master, Flaubert. Maurice Baring in *Have you Anything to Declare?* expresses the opinion that a beautiful anthology of French landscapes might be made from passages in Maupassant's stories and novels alone.

He quotes this winter scene as an example:

Un rideau de flocons blancs ininterrompu miroitait sans cesse en descendant vers la terre; il effaçait les formes, poudrait les choses d'une mousse de glace; et l'on n'entendait plus dans le grand silence de la ville calme et ensevelie sous l'hiver que ce froissement vague, innommable et flottant de la neige qui tombe, plûtot sensation que bruit, entremêlement d'atomes légers qui semblaient emplir l'espace, couvrir le monde.

This is not the language of the spoken word, but that of the written, of which Sir William Watson so well said: 'It does what the language of real life would do if it could. It speaks where the other mumbles; it is articulate where the other cannot out with its thoughts; it delivers the message which the other has dropped on the way.'

He was not the pupil of Flaubert for ten years without its affecting the construction of his sentences, and leaving a still deeper mark upon his style in other respects. It is true, as his friend Pol Neveux wrote in his preface to the Conard edition (on the whole the most balanced survey of Maupassant's life and works) that in his pages we do not discover phrases memorable out of their contexts, nor passages as unforgettable in rhythm as poetry. There are no sentences in his prose so superb as, to take one short example, the sentence:

Egypte! Egypte! tes grands Dieux immobiles ont les épaules blanchies par la fiente des oiseaux, et le vent qui passe sur le désert roule la cendre de tes morts.

The romantic passion of his 'irreproachable master' found no echo in his genius, but nevertheless through Flaubert something of Chateaubriand descended to Maupassant: a sense of the value of round vehement periods. It is this element in his style which is today in France and elsewhere out of favour, and masks from those to whom rhetoric is hateful, the value of that strong easy concision which made him master of the short story.

The long training to which Flaubert subjected him before he permitted him to publish, was to concentrate in description on whatever was salient in the object, and find for that the words which gave it the highest and most unmistakable relief. It was a training in harmony with the pupil's natural gift. In Maupassant the act of observation was simultaneous with analysis, or with—shall we call it that process of the mind which simplifies and defines the object? He was, therefore, able to present the figures in his stories with an authority and rapidity which no novelist, not even Balzac, has excelled; and to sketch in their settings in a few sentences. He thought with the eye—at least when he thought with most penetration. He was not a cultivated man; he read little. He brooded rather than thought. His close and devoted association with Flaubert may have reinforced his natural pessimism, his contempt for humanity and pity for its plight. This dark estimate of life was natural in him, though deepened by his own tragic fate: the madness of a terrible disease was lying in wait to spring like a beast from the jungle upon him. He feared it, dimly at first; then with an increasing horror for which the only poor relief was to be found either in violent distractions, restless travel, or the use of that fear itself as a theme for stories ('Le Horla', 'Lui', etc. etc.).

There is a saying which has won more complete assent than it deserves, that life is a comedy to those who think, a tragedy to those who feel. It seems to me truer, though less striking, to say that it is a comedy to those in whom an irrational fountain of gaiety incessantly plays, fed by a subconscious feeling of well-being and strength, as long as pain and sorrow do not come near enough to choke it. Men are so constituted that they can support with singular composure and courage the misfortunes of others. And though this is not an amiable trait, thanks to it much has been written which is of great benefit even to those who suffer. They have been helped by the strong and indifferent to laugh at many things which might otherwise have overwhelmed them.

The young Maupassant was endowed with an overplus of unreflective vitality. It is a commonplace of criticism to contrast the robust comedy of his early stories with the sombre and desperate note of despair and indignation which quivers through his later work. It was this that attracted to him Tolstoy, who was also born with a profound capacity for drawing instinctive rapture from the life of the body. He wrote upon Maupassant one of the most remarkable pieces of criticism of our times. He recognised in his work the born pagan who was left despairing, helpless, when the great god of youth deserted him. (Tolstoy did not know about the ancillary causes of that despair.) Reluctantly, painfully, this great enjoyer was compelled by his genius to testify to the emptiness of the purely instinctive life: such was Tolstoy's interpretation of Maupassant the writer. The mark of Maupassant's later work, his last novels (*Mont Oriol* is the turning-point), is an increased subjectivity. In *Fort Comme La Mort*, in *Notre Cœur*, he lost to a large extent his power of drawing characters with that sureness of touch and objectivity for which his earlier work is remarkable. The only characters who really live in them are those which are drawn from within, the heroes of those stories, who are Maupassant himself.

II

Henri-Rene-Albert-Guy de Maupassant was born on August 5th, 1850; perhaps (there is conflicting evidence) at the Château de Miromesnil, near Dieppe, in the chapel of which he was baptised. His family (not of the old *noblesse*) came from Lorraine, but had dwelt in Normandy since the middle of the eighteenth century: not, however, in that ornate and pleasing residence which his father hired shortly before Guy's birth and soon afterwards relinquished. The Maupassants were by no means well off. His boyhood was chiefly spent at Etretat and Fécamp, little places on the coast. He grew up a robust, muscular boy, taking his pleasures in out-of-door life, and in the company of peasants and fishermen whom he afterwards described so well, and of their children. Unlike the sons of the bourgeoisie, he was not class-conscious as far as such companions were concerned; and this upbringing helped to make him afterwards the kind of man whose servants are his friends. Bernard and Raymond, who managed his yacht, the *Bel-Ami*, adored him; and next to his mother and sister those two men were probably more distressed than other people when he went mad. Other people were chiefly inquisitive and excited when that happened.

His valet, François Tassart, who wrote an honest yet loyal book about his ten years' service (1883 to 1893), got better talk out of him than all but a very few friends. Maupassant would often share his impressions of men, women and places with François, but remain shut up like an oyster with most people. It is important to remember in drawing his character that he was the sort of virile man of whom those going with him for a day's shoot or a sail would be likely to say afterwards, 'that is a gentleman I like to work for'; or with whom any shepherd, peasant, old crone, farmer, fisherman, prostitute, house-drudge, would feel in a way at ease. In society, on the other hand, he was apt to be vulgar, dull, and boisterous—common. Yes, that's it, common.

He was fond of practical jokes too elaborate to be funny, and of boasting of his 'conquests' and priapean feats. In Paris, talking and behaving thus, he was naturally sometimes fooled himself: sent on spoof assignations to meet a countess or a famous actress who never turned up, or told to go in fancy dress to a party where all were in ordinary clothes. Whether during his last years of flaming notoriety he resented these tit-for-tats, I do not know. I think probably not. I suspect that he was then living in so bad a dream that even a humiliation was a welcome counter-irritant; as welcome as an unjust row over money with his devoted publisher. And if you imagine the disconcerting contrast between his behaviour, consonant only with rollicking youthful spirits, and the settled gloom in his eyes, and his sultry silences (Taine compared him to *un petit taureau triste*), you will probably conclude that it was not M. Guy de Maupassant's social gifts that led to his being pestered to death with invitations, but just society's snobbishness; and here and there, no doubt, the itch on the part of sophisticated women to experience the thrill of being under the scrutiny of a merciless writer.

Pestered to exasperation he certainly was, while his own contributions to social life consisted of entertainments designed to revive in himself the spirit of those bygone rowdy Sundays on the Seine, when he was a Civil Service clerk, with Mouche and 'les cinq papas': 'Petit Bleu', 'Tomahawk', 'Flat-cap', 'One-eye' and 'Plumtree' (Maupassant himself). He invited fast quasi-fashionable women to dinner with one other man, and the women would proceed to describe their husbands' tastes and behaviour in bawdy-houses; he taught the parrot in his boudoir to squawk 'Petit Cochon' as a greeting to any woman who came to see him; or he made it a condition of getting a schoolmistress a situation that she should first dress up as a pretty boy and nudge his other women guests under the table. He was not quick at discriminating between denizens of the *monde* and *demi-monde*, if both were richly dressed. In writing to Marie Bashkirtseff, he says that he has found it practical to pinch women at the opera: if that is taken in good part, he knows where he is; if it gives offence, he knows likewise.

All this is vulgar enough, like his own study in Paris, an etching of which is reproduced in that poor little book, M. George Normand's *La Fin de Maupassant.* His study recalls a line from Kipling's *The Mary Gloster*, 'And your rooms at College was beastly—more like a whore's than a man's.' Yes all vulgar enough; but even more desolating, when one recalls the depth of his feelings, the powers of his mind.

I think, too, we must imagine Maupassant in his relation to women during this period as in that predicament in which huntsmen with a reputation for hard riding find themselves when their nerve has begun, secretly, to fail.

In that room, however, with its podgy sofas and chairs, knick-knacks, perfumes, cushions, marquetry, and palms, he wrote with the regularity of a bank-clerk and the desperation of one working against time in a fading light; wrote, though often he could hardly see the words with his inflamed eyes, and though racked with headaches, which inhalations of ether temporarily relieved; wrote, taking down what, on one or two occasions, had seemed dictated to him by a fetch of himself seated on the other side of the table—that 'Lui' whom he so dreaded to find beside his fire when he returned alone to his rooms at night.

His output was enormous, earning unprecedented sums, though today they seem modest enough. (500 francs went a

long way in France in the 'eighties.) His novels sold quickly
by the sixty, seventy thousand. They went even better than the
collections of stories and sketches which, always first paid for
at record figures by editors, he garnered rapidly together in
volumes, sometimes publishing three in one year. He was as
much a king of railway bookstalls in his day as Edgar Wallace
ever was, but his books were not time-killers. True, much of
Maupassant's later work shows haste, and especially elaboration
of subject-matter which, when the influence of Flaubert was
stronger upon him, he would have rejected as trivial. Yet the
shadow of his beloved master was by his side, and this astonishing facility was the reward of ten years' apprenticeship. Maupassant still held, too, his master's creed that to be what one
may be, to master the instrument which is one's gift, to learn
to play on it to perfection is duty, conduct, everything—the
only success in life. It is a guiding principle with obvious
limitations, though nobler and with subtler and safer implications than most—than patriotism, for example; but it cannot
shore-up a tumbling life. Though Maupassant clung to it, the
exercise of his gift at last seemed also vanity.

There was a touch of *la folie de grandeur* in his behaviour,
which made the young Léon Daudet, for example, report after
meeting him that he seemed a strange mixture of genius, sick
man and ass. His disease made him extremely sensitive to cold;
his nerves to noises and crowds. Crowds are apt always to be
oppressive to those who have a low opinion of human nature,
but Maupassant's horror at finding himself in an audience or a
crush sometimes amounted to a phobia. He would chuck
everything and fly; solitude in open spaces beckoned like a
heavenly promise of peace. 'Anywhere, anywhere out of the
world.' And then to get away from women! A floating solitude
was best of all. He would, however, be careful, before starting,
to fix up an extremely lucrative contract for weekly sketches
and impressions, and it is to one of these flights that we owe
Sur l'eau. To earn more and more money became an increasing
necessity now. He had to keep up his little yacht; his flat in

Paris, a house at Etretat, a small villa near Cannes, and then there were his mother and his brother's family to help. In the confusion of his haunted life, his loyalty to such obligations remained as fixed as his habit of industry and his Norman cupidity.

Sur l'eau is the book which brings the reader nearest to Maupassant himself. He never wrote better than under the first intoxication of being alone, or more significantly than when the boon of solitude turned slowly to despair. Then the elemental poet is released in him; and that feeling of identity with earth, animals, and the instinctive life of men, doomed like the beasts, then finds an expression which can lend, occasionally, even to a trivial anecdote a certain grandeur. It is his jet-black pessimism that disinfects his vulgarity, his monkey-house view of sex, and excuses a laugh sometimes too contemptuous. A happy Maupassant would be as intolerable as that crass vulgarian Georges Daroy himself, the hero of *Bel-Ami*, with whom, by the way, he has some unpleasant affinities; but Maupassant alone with nature, himself, and human fate, appears to me lovable. Indeed, he attracts me so much that I am rather puzzled at it; and in case an analysis of my feelings towards him may lead others to examine theirs, I will attempt one.

In the first place I respond to his instinctive crude, direct, uncritical love of Life, and what accompanies that passion when strong (as smoke does fire), his resentment at decay and death. I love an author in whom, say, the spectacle of a school of porpoises plunging and turning in the sea, or of a stallion neighing and stamping in a field, rouses a kind of joy which is also, in some odd way, a fellow feeling.

Again only an author who is aware of the ridiculous and merciless egotism of human beings inspires me with confidence when he does draw attention to the strange intermittent nobility of human nature. When Maupassant melts or admires, I trust him; I am melted and I, too, admire. Then he has as a writer the master quality of sincerity; that is to say, he hates and loves genuinely. His moral sympathies are not always to be relied on; and, though everyone would prefer him to be always both refined and sincere, I would rather he were vulgar and sincere than only pretending, like most novelists, to have better preferences. Lastly, he has the great virtue of the pessimist, pity. His sense of the cruelty of nature and of man is as deep as his despair. He felt his own tragedy as part of the world's, and that is a mark of greatness.

HARDY

1940

SEVENTY YEARS have passed since Thomas Hardy wrote his first novel—years that have brought more changes into the world and our way of living than any other stretch of time of the same length. So Hardy, as a novelist, belongs to a different epoch, but his verse had affinities with later times— with poetry we label modern. The slow rhythm of old country life in England, the seclusion in which people lived, seeing only neighbours, are reflected in his leisurely stories. Nor were his characters pelted day in, day out, with scraps of miscellaneous knowledge; it was easier perhaps for those who were not foolish to be wise. All this gives an old-fashioned air to his fiction, refreshing to the reader, once the slowness of his story-telling and his simplification of character and motive are accepted.

He came of peasant stock, but his people, though from the squire's point of view villagers, were of that standing from which it is fairly easy for a clever son to rise in the world. His father was a builder; he worked with his own hands, but he was also an employer of labour. Hardy received a good education. He read good books as a child, learnt some Latin and a little Greek. His parents could, I think, have just afforded to send him to the University, say with the help of a small scholarship. But instead he was trained as an architect. In leisure hours he took to writing poetry. From poetry he turned to novel-writing, and after the publication of *Jude the Obscure* in 1896 (*Jude* was abused and the abuse disgusted and hurt him), he took to expressing himself only in verse, though he published one more novel which he had written earlier.

I remember his saying that it was the desire to make a little money that first made him turn to fiction. He had heard that Meredith, whom he knew as reader for Chapman and Hall, had made a hundred pounds by a novel—and he thought he would try to do the same. The result was *Desperate Remedies*, 1871. I should be surprised to hear that it earned that, but those with eyes might have seen in it (I don't think anybody did) that here was a writer who might learn to handle words so as to convey a new beauty and his own sense of life; who, to use his own words, was born 'to intensify the expression of things'. His second novel, *Under the Greenwood Tree*, a beautiful humorous little story published the following year, brought him recognition from writers like Leslie Stephen, and two years afterwards, with *Far from the Madding Crowd*, he began to capture the wider public—you see, he did not write long in obscurity.

Like Meredith, his great contemporary, Hardy belongs to the class of poet-novelists. Meredith in his novels dealt with the sunny side of life; Hardy with its shadows. There was little humour in Meredith, but much wit; Hardy is the reverse of a *clever* writer—but there is much delightful humour. His country folk have been compared with Shakespeare's rustics; and, personally, I often prefer them. They seem in touch with life in a deeper way; and though their minds are slow and cumbrous, their sense of words is delightful. In their talk there are long pauses of silence when heads are shaken over life and tankards drained. They've a great appreciation of silence as well as savoury phrases. Here is a scrap of the conversation of the Melstock choir in *Under the Greenwood Tree*:

'Yes, Geoffrey is a clever man if ever there was one. Never says anything; not he.'

'Never.'

'You might live wi' that man, my sonnies, a hundred years—and never know there was anything in him.'

'Ay, one of these up-country London ink-bottle fellers would call Geoffrey a fool.'

'Ye would never find out what's in that man—never.'

'Silent? Ah, he is silent. He can keep silence well.'

'That man's silence is wonderful to listen to.'

Hardy's themes are generally sad, both as poet and novelist. There are green isles of peace and happiness in his stories, but a greyness beats upon them and the ominous murmur of it is heard in their most sheltered recesses. Is this* the moment then, you may ask, to turn to *Tess of the D'Urbervilles, The Wood-landers, The Mayor of Casterbridge, The Return of the Native, Jude the Obscure?* Yes, I think so—it is the function of tragic literature to dignify sorrow and disaster.

A good many years ago I had the pleasure of seeing Hardy sometimes, of talking with him, and sometimes bicycling with him. His simplicity of feeling was more impressive in him than anything he actually said. A few characteristic things, however, I remember him saying. He had been reading or re-reading *Tom Jones* and referring to that character—the poor trollop in Tom Jones' village, Molly Seagrim, about whose humiliations there are many jokes—he said 'It's a most extra-ordinary thing but Fielding seems to have forgotten she was a woman.' I remember thinking at the time—'There speaks a man to whom village life is real in a very different degree to which it is to a writer of the squire-class like Fielding; and how characteristic too of one who never in his work forgets the pain and seriousness of life.'

Once when we were passing the scene of some incident in *Tess*, he said to me, 'If I had thought that story was going to be such a success I'd have made it a *really good book.*'

One other trifle comes back to me. He was telling me about Andrew Lang to whom he had been reconciled (Lang had written a cutting review of *Tess of the D'Urbervilles*). 'Oh he *was* a clever man. I never talked to a cleverer man. I suppose it's living in towns and talking that makes one like that. Do you think if I lived in London, I would become clever too?' I remember saying 'Clever people are as common as blackberries —I'm a clever man myself; I don't think you need bother about cleverness'—and we looked at each other and smiled.

Hardy's appearance is familiar from photographs and pic-

---

* 3rd June, 1940

tures. Two of the best known of his portraits, Augustus John's portrait of him and Strang's etching, do not seem to me like him. I do not recognise in the John portrait that startled and supercilious stare. There is far too much vigour and not nearly enough delicacy in the face, and the same comment applies, in my opinion, to the etching. There was something far more odd, winning and somehow twisted both in his features and expression; something agelessly elfin in him which neither artist has caught, and a glint in his eye which one might have associated with slyness in a mindless and insensitive man. He was very small, very quiet, self-possessed and extraordinarily unassuming. I seem to remember that his laughter made no sound. As is usual with subtle people, his voice was never loud and a gentle eagerness which was very pleasing, showed in his manner when he wanted sympathy about some point. He would instantly recoil on being disappointed. I observed in him once or twice a look, a movement, too slight to be called a wince, but not unlike the almost imperceptible change one sees in a cat when a gesture has perturbed it.

Hardy the novelist and Hardy the poet are the same man, though people differ as to whether his verse excels his prose. Certainly as he grew older he himself came to prefer the condensation of verse, but he did not keep poetry to express only the more intense and rarer kinds of emotion. That's where he is akin to modern poets. Many of his poems were on subjects he might have treated in a story—that vivid and moving ballad 'A Tramp-Woman's Tragedy', for example. He constantly noted in verse the same kinds of incident he makes important in his novels. It is a dangerous thing for a poet to attempt, but Hardy could afford to because of the great seriousness of his attention. If his poetry was often that of a novelist, his novels were always those of a poet—put it like that, if you like. In both is the same profoundly tragic, wistful, watchful response to life. Much of his work is an austere but gentle descent upon the dust and ashes of things, of the fragility of love, and the perversities of fate. Unwelcome truths, but old truths, and

Hardy presented them with a consciousness of their gravity. 'The solemnity of earth, its woods and fields, and lonely places, has passed into his work; and when he takes it in hand, to deal with the passions of men, that spirit guides and directs him.'

His work has weaknesses. His writing is sometimes clumsy and pedantic. He will say, for instance, 'every point in the milkmaid became a deep rose colour' when he meant that she blushed; or speak of 'atmospheric cutlery' instead of a sharp wind. He has written exquisite meditative lyrics, but also some which are more like tunes played on a snoring old 'cello.

If you listen to such criticism, and a true admirer always listens to the other side, don't forget that no fault-finding can reach that high simplicity which underlies Hardy's work, and is one of the marks of fine literature. It may sink into mere naïvety in places; that tragic sense may here and there sag into a too-easy and passive a melancholy, but it is there—this profound sense of man's destiny and of the turning of the wheel of fate.

JAMES JOYCE

1941

I

JAMES JOYCE was one of the writers (French and English) about whose fate we felt anxious when Paris fell; and now he is dead—after escaping first to unoccupied France and thence, a sick man, to Switzerland; and after sufferings we know as yet nothing about, though we can infer that something equivalent to destitution was one of them.

Poverty in the shape of sordid embarrassments he had been used to in childhood, youth, and early middle-age, and he had learnt how to deal with it by closing the petals of his mind tighter and tighter over the seed-bearing centre of his being—his life as an artist. He defended himself by exalting confidence to a pitch of self-centred arrogance. This proved good for his originality though bad for the content-value of his work, for it accentuated the narrowness of his intensity.

He came to believe (so I read the chart of his literary production) that he contained the world in himself, and therefore that by sinking an ever-deepening shaft into his own consciousness he would reach the all-embracing. His genius ceased altogether to be fed from outside. Nothing is more obvious in his work than its entire dependence on early impressions, preserved in a memory of unrivalled vividness and exactitude.

Dublin, Dublin, Dublin—it never gets away from what Joyce saw and felt in Dublin in boyhood and youth. Nothing happened to him—as an artist—after that; no further experience enriched his imagination or widened the range of his sympathies. Most writers sooner or later put up the shutters, so to speak, and live upon previous accumulations; but this happened very early with Joyce. He is a still more glaring example of it than Swinburne. Like Swinburne, but to a far greater extent, he became more and more absorbed in words: in the beginning there was life, in the end was only 'the word'. Now and then he read an author—Vico, for example, whose thought influenced him; but development was chiefly in the direction of linguistics.

After the shutters have gone up every artist becomes more exclusively interested in technique, in *how* to do things rather than in *what* to do. And with Joyce this absorption in technique became extravagantly extreme owing to the direction of his creative impulse, which was to sink that shaft into his own subconscious, regardless of whether the matter reached thereby became more and more personal and incommunicable. He became entirely absorbed in this feat of mental engineering, inventing a language fully intelligible only to himself and in scraps and at *moments* to a few devoted admirers, who had been furnished with hints. The world to which that shaft led down was as isolated as that of a madman, to whom everything has an intense private significance. (See *Finnegans Wake*.)

When *Ulysses* first appeared I wrote a few notes on it in *The New Statesman*, and the following passage is of interest as recording a first impression:

Mr James Joyce's *Ulysses* strikes me as less important as a work of art than as a symptom. For pages and pages it is nearly unreadable, making the reader ache with boredom; but it contains more artistic dynamite than any book published for many years. That dynamite is placed under the modern novel. . . . The modern novelist flatters himself that he interprets the drift of thoughts and feelings through the heads of his characters, and here Mr Joyce undercuts him completely. I cannot conceive the modern novelist who is capable of grasping the merits of this work, and at the same time comprehending its nullity, not being utterly discouraged.

I came to put a higher value on Joyce's originality, which required more rapid readjustments than I could make at once; but the above passage contains a point to which I still adhere.

Joyce's influence is chiefly confined to writers or potential writers; for however much opinions may differ as to the value of his work, Joyce's extraordinary virtuosity and originality cannot be disputed. He began as a realist with *Dubliners* (a volume of short stories); and whenever he has chosen to evoke concrete things he has had at his service a visualising power of extraordinary intensity and an enormous vocabulary. During the first world war he published *A Portrait of the Artist as a Young Man*: there we were planted deep in the centre of an adolescent mind; we caught vivid glimpses of the external world and heard scraps of talk through the curtain of the young man's moods —dark, thick, oppressive. There was a beauty in the book as of a dawn struggling behind rain; and also horror in it as of actual physical birth. Nor was the creature born the artist—perfect and free; rather he was a being *maimed, solitary,* and *sullen.* Stephen Daedalus, the hero of the *Portrait,* is also the second most important character in *Ulysses.*

Now, whatever the future verdict may be with regard to the merits of *Ulysses*; whether it agrees with that of some of the younger English writers and critics, namely that it is *the* masterpiece of modern fiction, or whether, as others have concluded, in spite of the author's extraordinary linguistic gifts, it is a failure as a work of art; of *one* thing there can be no doubt —*it is a most extraordinary and original work.*

Readable from end to end it certainly is *not*, except by those interested in literary technique. It is, as you probably know, an enormously lengthy account of *one* day in the life of one man, a Jewish commercial traveller in Dublin; that is to say, it purports to be a record, together with his conversations and chance meetings with others, of *all* that passed through his mind. Different devices of style are used with great skill to convey different states of consciousness, and the thoughts of Bloom and the incidents which take place follow the same orders as events remotely analogous to them in the Odyssey! This correspondence is the *pattern*—extraordinarily intricate and *artificial*—into which Joyce's researches into the backward abysses of consciousness are woven. Why, I have never understood. To give form to the formless, I suppose; but such a form is too external to the substance. It is imposed from without and to my mind adds nothing but pedantry to the book.

You would think that *Ulysses* must be a terminal product, that it was impossible to get closer to the texture of consciousness than Joyce had done in certain passages. Language itself is a convention, a communal product—not the product of a single mind, and though words can be used to convey subjective impressions, they only do so on condition that their meaning, however vague, is agreed upon. Joyce's methods in *Ulysses* of representing a stream of consciousness were really just as conventional as the traditional ones of condensing the contents of somebody's mind at a certain moment. His were more vaporous, that was all. Where the traditional novelist would have described a few vague images that floated through Bloom's mind during a short snooze after flirting with Girty Macdowell, Joyce conveyed them thus:

We two naughty Grace darling she him half-past the bed met him pike hoses frillies for Raoul to perfume your wife black hair heave under embon senorita young eyes Mulvey plump years dream return tail and Agendath swooney lovely. . . .

Here each word has an associated connection in Bloom's mind with the one before, and if you *can* remember all that has happened to Bloom during the preceding hours, you may be able to see why. But what a tiresome method of conveying the sensation of a snooze! Moreover, it is still far from really recording accurately a streamy-dreamy state of semiconsciousness.

Joyce seems to have felt this, and proceeded to manufacture a composite language. Fragments of what was after many years published as *Finnegans Wake* appeared under the head of 'Work in Progress'. In these by means of rhythms (of which he was a master), assonances, puns, and portmanteau-words formed out of the pickings of many languages, slang, Dublin catches, the clues to which composites often none but himself knew, he endeavoured to weave a net of sounds in which to catch the essentially ungraspable, ever-melting stream of consciousness.

I have not met anyone who has read *Finnegans Wake*; dipped

into with enthusiasm, yes, but not read it. Was Joyce's literary
life, then, a failure? No: he remains in the first place 'damned
good to steal from'. In the second, now and then a vague majestic
beauty glides ghostlike through the bewildering darkness, as in
Ulysses. In the third, he worked out to the last limit a direction
of lingual exploration which writers are constantly tempted to
follow in the hope of treasure trove. Henceforth they will know
more clearly how far they can go without losing touch with
everything—except their own solitary minds.

II

I wish I could meet someone who knew James Joyce well.
The best substitute I have found for that is John Eglinton's
Irish Portraits (Macmillan), which contains a good description
of Joyce in his youth in Dublin before he emigrated. But
although Mr Eglinton is a good observer, he was looking at his
subject from a distance. His impressions are of value, but they
do not help me to solve the problem which bothers me, *why* a
writer like Joyce spent the last fifteen years or so of his life in
writing endless pitch-dark rigmaroles in a private language,
brightened by a few amusing puns. What made him do it?
What was the psychological impulse behind the pedantic and
elaborate stuff he called in the end *Finnegans Wake*? Had he
any doubts?

Light upon the last point—a gleam, I did find in a book
called *Being Geniuses Together*, by Mr Robert McAlmon, an
American writer (published by Secker and Warburg). This is
a piece of autobiography, entertaining in a downright, hard-
boiled way, which makes the reader think he ought to know a
good deal more about Mr McAlmon than I do for one. Mr
McAlmon saw a good deal of Joyce in post-war Paris days,
both before and after the publication of *Ulysses*. He was one
of those who used to accompany him on his periodic 'binges'.
He knew Joyce drunk as well as sober, and apparently the no-
nonsense directness of Mr McAlmon was a relief to Joyce after

the gaping worship with which he was surrounded—anyhow, Joyce seems to have been open with McAlmon, whatever his opinion of him as a writer may have been.

For a good many years Miss Harriet Weaver, who ran the Egoist Press, subsidised Joyce. It is due to her that he was able to concentrate upon writing *Ulysses*; afterwards profits from it enabled him to live with an easy margin. Two passages in *Being Geniuses Together* (note the touch of irony in the title) struck me as being of interest to a critic. The first concerns the part played by Mr McAlmon in the creation of the famous monologue of Mrs Bloom with which *Ulysses* ends.

Now, the husband of the English typist in Paris, to whom Joyce had handed the MS., had destroyed some forty pages of the original script because it was obscene. Not wanting that to happen again, Joyce asked Mr McAlmon to type the fifty last pages.

The next day he gave me the handwritten script, and his handwriting is minute and hen-scrawly; very difficult to decipher. With the script he gave me some four notebooks, and throughout the script were marks in red, yellow, blue, purple and green, referring me to phrases which must be inserted from one of the notebooks. For about three pages I was painstaking, and actually re-typed one page to get the insertions in the right place. After that I thought 'Molly might just as well think this or that a page or two later or not at all', and made the insertions wherever I happened to be typing. Years later upon asking Joyce if he'd noticed that I'd altered the mystic arrangement of Molly's thought, he said that he had, but agreed with my viewpoint. Molly's thoughts were irregular in several ways at best.

This is illuminating. The ruminations of Mrs Bloom have been considered a triumph of subtle art. If Mr McAlmon is to be trusted, this shows that where the inner monologue is concerned it does not matter much what branching association an author follows; a typist's alterations may pass, even with the author, as 'insight'.

The second significant passage refers to a much later date, when *Finnegans Wake*, under the heading of 'Work in Progress', had been appearing in M. Jolas's magazine *Transition* for some years. But first let me quote what appears to me a good comment. It is a comparison between Joyce's work and that of Miss Gertrude Stein:

They are as unlike as the North Pole is from the Equator. Joyce knows words, their rhythms, colour, associations, capacity to evoke, their histories and their emotional significations. Stein fumbles and mauls them, and gradually something emerges as so much mud emerges into some sort of form in the hands of a maladroit child. Stein's wit is sluggish; Joyce's is almost too quick, constant, and, around a limited range of experience, variable. They have in common only a tendency to withdraw themselves from the horde, to make themselves precious, but that tendency is indeed light with Joyce, and would not be in him at all if it were not that his eyes do not allow him to be as gregariously free and easy as he would like to be. He is not afraid of being unmasked, for he is sure of himself, and I have never known him to boast without immediately withdrawing it in a 'what do we all know about it' manner. That cannot be said of poor Gertrude.

Apparently Joyce had doubts about his final manner. One day he asked Mr McAlmon, 'Do you think I may be on the wrong track with my *Work in Progress*? Miss Weaver says she finds me a mad man. Tell me frankly. No man can say for himself.' Mr McAlmon says that it was one of his 'kindly days', and that he assured him that he was only 'just touched enough for genius in the James Joyce manner'.

Here is the significant passage:

When the Quinn collection of manuscripts were sold the one of *Ulysses* brought a surprisingly low price, but Joyce said resignedly, 'Probably they are right. Who can say what the next generation will think of me? What do we think of the great men of the past generation?'

Now he declares that he is tired of hearing about *Ulysses*. There has been too much said about the book. When I suggest that perhaps in *Dubliners* there is writing of his much more apt to last, he does not disagree, and wonders also if he might not have developed that style of writing rather than going into words too entirely. It was his eye-sight, his inability to keep on reading freely, his incapacity to drink much without paying too great a price as regards his health, and his poverty, and the war, that decided many things which relate to his style and approach to writing. Nevertheless, his infatuation with words was born within him.

Joyce was, of course, not mad; but the immense importance he gave in his later writings to chance associations—usually they were merely verbal—is a characteristic of certain types of madness; and the arrogance with which he demanded that the reader should take the trouble to discover them, even if that implied learning Esquimaux words as well as those of a dozen other languages, comes near megalomania. In *Anna Livia Plurabelle*, that fragment of *Finnegans Wake* which, when rendered on a gramophone record of his soothing Irish-tenor voice, certainly does evoke melopoetically the sensations of endless flowing night, peace, death, he boasted that he had inserted cross-references to the names of a hundred rivers, and that in its word-distortions there were hints of the word Peace in twenty-nine languages.

Now to think that a melopoetic effect is increased by an echo of a language in which the reader is not thinking, or with which he is, perhaps, entirely unfamiliar, is, to say the least, absurd; and Joyce, who was, in addition to all his gifts, a clever man, would have never supposed so, had he not been converted to a theory which the French call 'The mysticism of the word', the belief that it is through acquaintance with *words* and knowledge of how to arrange them, that we reach comprehension of life. It is a theory that dates from Mallarmé and Rimbaud. It has influenced our own 'modern' poetry. Joyce was the end of a movement, not the beginning of one.

Concerning the seriousness with which he took verbal associations, let me repeat a story: Mr Frank O'Connor calling on him in Paris noticed a picture of Cork in a very odd frame. 'Yes', said Joyce, 'I had the greatest difficulty in getting that frame, but naturally a view of Cork could only be framed in cork.'

A very large part of *Finnegans Wake*, and the explanation of it, are implicit in that reply, which was not intended as a joke.

LERMONTOV

circa 1942

FOR nearly all readers everywhere (even in Russia itself)
Russian literature begins in the nineteenth century. It is
the youngest literature in Europe, and it opened with what
has been called 'The Golden Age of Russian Poetry' and the
publication of Pushkin's first book of verse in 1820. Pushkin
is to the Russians what Dante is to Italians and Goethe to
Germans. And as the English may sometimes speak of Shakespeare and Milton together, but without intending either to
compare them or assert their equality, so for many years
Russians coupled with Pushkin's name that of Lermontov.

This 'Golden Age' soon ended. It was followed by the era of
the great Russian novelists, which was of far more importance
to the world at large; for poetry—and this is most apt to be
true of the best—may be impossible to translate. In 1837
Pushkin was killed in a duel at the age of 35; and this catas-
trophe was, as we shall see, a turning-point in the career of the
younger poet, Lermontov. He also was killed in a duel, and
when he was only 27.

Lermontov was born in Moscow in 1814. He was the son of
a poor army officer who was descended from a Scot, one George
Learmont, who in 1613 had entered first the Polish then the
Russian army as a soldier of fortune. His father had made a
runaway match with a romantic girl belonging to a wealthy
landed family. His mother died in the third year of a probably
not very happy marriage, and her aristocratic mother adopted
the future poet. Afterwards she did all in her power to alienate
him from his father whom he adored.

Nothing can make childhood more unhappy, or is more likely
to throw children back upon themselves than enmity between
those on whom they are dependent for love, and Lermontov's

childhood seems to have been sad, lonely, and dreamy. But
his grandmother saw to it that he should have a good education.
In those days, and indeed for many years after that date, the
culture of the upper classes in Russia was European. Children
of the aristocracy were brought up to speak French to their
parents and were taught English or German by tutors or
governesses. The little Lermontov was very clever, and he
soon mastered those three languages. His first verses, composed
at the age of 14, were written in French. (So by the way were
Pushkin's.) And in his maturity he was to translate into
Russian verse some of Byron's poetry, notably 'The Dying
Gladiator'. This mention of Byron is important. From early
years he read Byron with intense delight; and when we examine
Lermontov's poetry and the temper of his mind, we see that
he has affinities with that proud egotistic poet who had so much
influence (though there was nothing of the democrat in him)
upon continental rebels. Byron was the loudest voice in that
romantic movement in literature which became closely connected with the revolutions, whether frustrated or successful,
of '48.

Lermontov reminds us of Byron at several points. When he
was ten he was taken to the Caucasus, the scenery of which he
was to describe so perfectly in prose and verse. There he fell
in love with a little girl of his own age. 'I have never loved in
the same way since', he afterwards declared. Oddly enough,
such a precocious amorous experience also finds a parallel in
the childhood of Byron. But the resemblance between Lermontov's heroes and those of Byron is far more striking than
such coincidences.

The figure that fascinated their imaginations and inspired
much of their verse was a strange being, aloof and disillusioned,
contemptuous and fearless, but capable of exercising an irresistible charm over others. In the love of women such a figure
sought relief from his loneliness, but always in vain. Experience
of love only added to his melancholy a sombre or cynical regret
that he had shattered the happiness of some trivial but lovely

creature, and convinced him that he was himself *un homme fatal.*

Now anybody can see the relation of such a figure to the day-dreams of thwarted adolescence. Intermittently both poets tried to behave like their heroes in real life. 'My youthful mind was troubled', wrote Lermontov, 'by a mighty figure among other visions. Like a king he blazed forth proud and taciturn, but with a magic sweetness that inspired awe. My spirit shuddered, and the wild vision haunted my mind for years, but I left him at last for other dreams.' Yet not before he had inspired verse which, as with Byron, made the poet famous. In his great novel, *A Hero of our Time,* published a year before his death, Lermontov detached himself from his lurid day-dream hero and saw around him. Pechorin in that story is a figure rooted in realities. Lermontov's enemies said Pechorin was a portrait of the author. Lermontov replied: 'The hero of our time is indeed a portrait but not of a single man; it is the portrait of the vices of our generation.' He added that the book 'disclosed the illness from which this generation suffers'. He had turned from day-dreams to diagnosis.

At first sight it seems strange that aristocratic poets like Byron and Lermontov, who with their scorn for humanity were so proud of their own despair, should have inspired reformers and rebels. The explanation lies in their proud individualism. It made them passionate after freedom and resentful of authority; while their scorn fell first upon those immediately surrounding them, upon the privileged, the frivolous, and powerful. Recall Byron's attacks upon the Tory Party, on George III, on Castlereagh, and even the British national hero, Wellington. In Lermontov this defiant spirit showed itself early. At the age of 17 he was dismissed without a degree from Moscow University for protesting against the incompetence of the professors. He then enlisted and, after being trained at a military school in St. Petersburg, became at 18 an officer in the Hussars. During the next five years, with an allowance of a thousand a year, he led a life of fashion. But, like Byron, he was both bored by society and gnawed by a

misgiving that his pose as a stony-hearted Dandy of Sorrows
was only half sincere and not always impressive. He proclaimed
his grief and resented sympathy: 'Don't seek to pity me!' he
said, 'Since I despise my own sufferings, what are those of
others to me?'

Like Byron he tried sensuality and light loves as a cure. In
1833 he wrote to a friend that his life of dreams was now over:
'un bonheur palpable, qui ne fasse que tromper mes sens en
laissant mon âme tranquille et inactive', was what he was
seeking. That expedient, too, was to fail him. Meanwhile
between 1828 and 1832 he had written out of his dreams and
despair most of those early lyrics, which later were to become
famous, and many of which are fascinating and beautiful. He
was very critical of his early work, but the note of Byronic
disillusionment instantly awoke echoes in others:

> We drink the cup of life while yet
>   A veil our eyes are keeping;
> And the cup's golden brim is wet
>   With tears of our own weeping.
>
> But when the veil falls from our eyes,
>   As Death appears before us,
> Then with the veil the mystery flies
>   That held enchantment o'er us.
>
> Oh then we see the golden cup
>   Was empty in its gleaming,
> That only dreaming filled it up,
>   Nor even ours the dreaming!
>
>   (*Translated by* Sir Maurice Bowra)

But he was not famous yet; he was only 22. Then, in 1837,
Pushkin was killed in a duel. Suddenly impersonal grief
mastered him. Moreover it was a grief mixed with intense
indignation. The sneers he overheard of people connected with
the Court roused him to fury, and he added to his lament in
memory of the great poet, some twenty lines or so, composed,
it is said, in hardly more than the same number of minutes.
These lines became famous. Here is a paraphrase of them:

But you who stand, a haughty crowd, round the throne, you hang men of genius and famous champions of freedom! Now, the law protects you, And justice dare not open her lips. But God's verdict stands—you pack of dissolute creatures! A stern judge is waiting for you. The clink of your gold will not buy Him.... And even the spilling of your black blood will not cleanse the stain of the pure poet's which you have shed.

These lines travelled from lip to lip in St. Petersburg, and manuscript copies of them circulated in Russia. The Czar was asked to punish him and Lermontov was sentenced not to Siberia (thanks to his influential relations), but to one year's exile in the Caucasus; a mild sentence. This exile proved a blessed event. It enabled him to describe, with an unrivalled exact impressiveness, in verse and prose, those grand mountains and forests. Moreover, the Caucasian mountain tribes were then fighting for their independence against the Russians with a tenacity which appealed to his love of wildness and freedom. Lermontov expressed these sympathies in two long poems. 'Mtsyri' is the cry of a young soul longing for liberty. It is the story of a Circassian village boy brought up in a Russian monastery. The monks think they have subdued his primitive instincts and his love of home; but he escapes one stormy night while they are praying in church. 'As for me, I was like a wild beast', the boy is made to say afterwards. 'I was prepared to fight storm and lightning and the tiger of the forest.' But he is feeble and cannot make his way home. An old monk finds him dying from injuries he got while struggling with a leopard. 'You want to know what I did while I was free,' he says to the old man who tends his wounds. 'I *lived*! And but for those three days my life would have been more empty than your powerless old age. Thou art old and grey, and long for nothing now. No matter! Thou hast lived—once. I might have lived myself.' Being young he hates to die.

Lermontov's other long poem of this period, 'The Demon', is even more romantic and more distinctly Byronic. It is the story of the love of a sort of supernatural 'Manfred' for a Georgian maid who takes refuge in a convent when the Demon has used his powers to murder by the hand of robbers her peasant bridegroom. The poem is in part a description of the emotions of a superhuman being condemned by his nobler qualities, as well as his baser ones, to frustration and torment. Demonic man and angelic woman (such was its heroine Tamara), are characteristic figures of the Romantic Movement. The verse of this narrative poem is extremely musical. Kropotkin, in his history, *Ideals and Realities of Russian Literature*, therefore compares Lermontov with Shelley rather than with Byron; both in respect of his verse and (though this seems more doubtful) also in spirit. He loved Lermontov, and liked to think that he chiefly resembled the more disinterested and humanitarian poet. 'Lermontov's demonism or pessimism', he wrote, 'was not the pessimism of despair, but a militant protest against all that is ignoble in life . . . the irritation of a strong man at seeing others round him so weak and so base.' To an idealistic revolutionary of the nineteenth century like Kropotkin, who was also nearer in date to Lermontov himself, this might well seem a better reading of the poet. But Russians of a later generation have taken a different view. Prince Mirsky, who before his return to Soviet Russia was for some years professor of Russian Literature at London University, wrote in his preface to the translation by Reginald Merton (by the way a good one) of *A Hero of our Time* (Philip Allan, 1928), 'Within the last fifty years, Lermontov's poetry has lost much of its attraction for us'. If effective, 'The Demon' strikes modern Russians as somewhat 'crudely rhetorical'. It no longer seems, as it did to their grandfathers, 'the acme of the poetical'. 'But', Mirsky continued, 'beneath the tinsel is a poetic energy. It may be a sea of undistilled emotion and rhetoric, but here and there emerge island peaks that alone perhaps in the whole of Russian literature rise into the golden and purple spheres of genuine romantic vision. While in his last years he was rapidly casting off the old scales of rhetorical romanticism, and, stimulated by the example of Pushkin, forging a new realistic style of poetry which, alas, was not destined to attain full maturity.'

Lermontov returned from exile to find himself famous. 'But what he had hinted at in his poetry' (Mirsky is thinking of his 'Duma', those satirical reflections in verse which led to his being exiled to the Caucasus a second time) 'he had already achieved in a novel.' *A Hero of our Time* was published in 1840, a year before his death. 'It is difficult', this admirable critic adds, 'to speak with moderation of this marvellous book. Its principal charms, the unique quality of its style, is not, of course, transferable into another language. It is the perfection of Russian prose.' This style is transparent and cool, like the mountain air of the regions it describes. Nevertheless, a good deal of its charm does get through Merton's translation. We come to know the characters, thanks to a clear description of what they do and how they behave; and one character, old Maxim Maximych, is clearly the forerunner of those Russian officers whom Tolstoy afterwards drew so well in *War and Peace*. Chekov, though his awareness of what was false in Lermontov's romanticism is shown in Solyany in *The Three Sisters* (a character who delights to fancy himself like Lermontov), thought the episode called 'Taman' in *A Hero of our Time* the finest short story ever written.

It is interesting that the quarrel which led to the duel in which Lermontov lost his life, was excited by his outspoken contempt for a romantic pose in another man; and also that, most strangely, Lermontov had anticipated his own fate in an early poem called 'The Dream'.

> By hot noon, in a vale of Dargestan,
> Lifeless, a bullet in my breast, I lay;
> Smoke rose from a deep wound, and my blood ran
> Out of me, drop by drop, and ebbed away.
>
> I lay upon the burning sand alone.
> Sheer precipices crowded all around.
> Their yellow tops were scorching in the sun,
> And I scorched too, in death's sleep, on the ground.

. . . .

She dreamed she saw a vale of Dargestan . . .
There on the slope a well-known body lay;
Smoke rose from a black wound, and the blood ran
In cold streams out of it, and ebbed away.

What passed in that lonely spot in the Caucasus where the
duellists faced each other on that fatal day has been recorded:
how Lermontov fired first and in the air, and how his adversary
then took so long an aim, while the poet stood scornful and
composed, that the seconds almost stopped the duel. Lermontov
fell dead, shot through the breast.

Nothing helps us more towards understanding a great
foreign writer's talent than to follow the vicissitudes of his fame
among his own countrymen. I have already quoted Kropotkin
and Mirsky. Quite early in the twentieth century Lermontov
was attacked by Solovyov for his lack of humility. He was
answered by Merejkowski, whose book on *Dostoievsky and
Tolstoy* is well known in England and America; his reply is
a defence of Lermontov's pride and of Lermontov the rebel.

'We have been taught', Merejkowski wrote of his countrymen in 1909, 'to submit by nature and by history; by Byzantine
Monks, Tartar Khans, Moscow Tzars, Petersburg Emperors—
daily executioners. All Russian literature is busy teaching us
humility. Pushkin wrote his Ode to Liberty—and gave in;
Gogol wrote Part I of *Dead Souls* and burned the MS. of
Part II—thus tacitly submitting to the principle of serfdom;
Dostoievsky revolted and went to Siberia—to return as a
prophet of humility; Tolstoy revolted and ended by preaching
non-resistance to evil. . . . There is but one Russian writer
who never gave in to his last breath: Lermontov, the Cain of
Russian Literature, was killed by the Abel of humility.'

This passage written, as you see, years before the Russian
Revolution, yet long after romanticism had become old-
fashioned, shows how a true poet will always be re-interpreted
by his posterity. If only he has written well, those who come
after him, however different they may be, will find fresh
reasons for admiring him again.

LANDOR

1942

LANDOR'S place in Literature is one of great mark and dignity. 'I neither am,' he said, 'nor shall ever be popular. Such was never my ambition. But one thing is quite certain. I shall have as many readers as I desire to have in other times than ours. I shall dine late; but the dining-room will be well lighted, the guests few and select.'

Born seventeen years before Shelley, he was the classical contemporary of the great romantic poets; dying in '64, the contemporary of Browning, Tennyson, and the Pre-Raphaelites. Landor's is the longest reign in English literary history. In a letter written to Lord Houghton from Florence in 1864, Swinburne says, 'I should like to throw up all other things on earth and devote myself to playing valet to him for the rest of his days. I would black his boots if he were *chez moi*. He has given me the shock of adoration which one feels at thirteen towards great men.'

The fruit of that visit was the beautiful valedictory in *Poems and Ballads*. Gosse, in his Life of Swinburne, notes the influence of Landor upon him. In some respects they were temperamentally akin. Both were aristocratic-republicans; both were alike in a far-fetched loyalty and wild chivalry overruling all sense of fairness to others—if need be. It may well have been Landor's example which first encouraged Swinburne to indulge in enormities of vituperation and stupendities of praise, though exercise in both those directions was to him (and would it not be also to us, had we the gift?) congenitally delightful. 'A rib of Shakespeare would have made a Milton, the same portion of Milton all the poets ever born since', or the phrase, 'songsters of goose-grazed commons', have a thoroughly Swinburnian ring, though both were written by Landor. Dickens caricatured Landor, whom he loved, as Boythorn in *Bleak House*. The picture of Mr Boythorn seated bolt-upright, storming violently, with an unruffled pet canary on his shoulder, caught a penetrating likeness. How happy, too, is the name Boythorn, suggesting, as it does, a character at once sturdy and prickly, and also (here lies the insight) a man in many ways permanently immature.

Landor wrote copiously, magnificently, waywardly, in prose and verse. His prose fills sixteen large volumes in Earle Welby's fine edition, to which Mr Stephen Wheeler afterwards added three of verse.

He is one of those writers for whom, if you care at all, you care immensely. His prose, apart from its content, gives me more pleasure than that of almost any other writer. The Landorian period is built up of chiselled statements, without conjunctions or transitions; the blocks, as Sidney Colvin pointed out, are so hard and well-cut that they require no mortar. Great splendour in emphasis and great composure in tone are the characteristics of this prose; and when the reader's mood is one in which contemplation is a state of recognition rather than of wonder; when his imagination does not hunger after either realism or mystery, but is content to rest in what is presented to it with perfect clarity and dignity, then he will not complain that Landor's pathos does not always move, that his invective does not often kill, that the famous characters in his *Conversations* have little individuality, and that Landor himself is a man of thoughts rather than a thinking man. For every sentence will conciliate his ear, every image will delight him, and each word contribute by its beautiful precision to some clear idea: 'I hate false words, and seek with care, difficulty and moroseness [how every writer must love him for adding 'moroseness'!] *those that fit the thing*.'

To learn to appreciate Landor is a classical education. Who ever forgets, once he has read it, Boccaccio's descriptions in the *Imaginary Conversations* of his meeting with Fiammetta in a dream, and of her offering him the cold cup of forgetfulness?

How admirable, too, is Landor's critical sententiousness: 'Poetry has no golden mean: mediocrity is here of another metal'; or, 'Nothing is easier than to catch the air of originality'; or, speaking of a certain kind of poetry, 'It has all the merits of a pocket handkerchief that smells of roses'; or, 'Truth, like the sun, coming down upon us too directly, may give us brain fever'; or, 'Fleas know not whether they are on the body of a giant or upon one of ordinary stature'; or the famous dictum, 'Clear writers like clear fountains do not seem as deep as they are: the turbid look most profound'; and in a 'debunking' age, what could be more salutary than to be reminded of this danger: 'We must not indulge in unfavourable views of mankind. By doing so we make bad men believe that they are no worse than others, and we teach the good that they are good in vain.'

Landor may not be a thinker, but how deep are his detached thoughts! He wrote many a page that was as lifeless as it was flawless. The amber of his style also embalmed mere flies and straws. Like several others who have mastered a manner of pronounced aesthetic quality, he sometimes ceased to observe its unfitness to the matter in hand; yet how frequently, both in prose and verse, Landor triumphed in the controlled expression of tenderness and solemnity!

WALT WHITMAN

1945

THIS is not an attempt to weigh Whitman in a balance, to see all round him or to compare him with this writer or that, pointing out where he excels or is excelled. Like all great men dead for some time he has been thoroughly criticised; for the world cannot for long remain blind to such a writer. All that can be said against that loose rhythmical form in which he expressed himself has been said—by poets too— by Swinburne, Meredith in particular (Meredith in a sonnet which he called 'The Orson of the Muse'—that is to say, the strong primitive man of poetry); and, on the other hand, men like Edward Carpenter with temperaments akin to Whitman's have explained how perfectly that form fitted what Whitman wanted to express. Whoever wishes to see exactly where Whitman stands as poet when he is judged from the point of view of imaginative tradition, let him read Santayana's essay on him in *Poetry and Religion*. Tried by Santayana's test he cannot be included among the greater poets—the very few. Not because he expressed the elemental instead of the conventional. No—not at all, but because the elements to which he reduced experience are chiefly moods and particular things. The majority of famous poets get no further than reducing experience to passions and characters, passions which are regarded as their own excuse for being; and these poets, too, from the philosopher's point of view—put beside those few who have had a steady sense of perfection in their conception of human life—show up also as lesser poets. Of course, it cannot be claimed for Whitman that he is among the great philosophical poets or that even one of his poems can rank among the best poems in the world. And yet there is not a writer some people would miss more if he had never lived or

132

never written—and I am one of those readers. Therefore I like
to remind others from time to time of qualities in Walt Whitman
which make him one whom it is good to be near, especially
these days, when many people find that war, bombs and
horrors have put a great space between them and some of the
literature they used to enjoy. Today, people often feel distressed when they are alone, and rely on reading, which may be
compared to a back seat on a witch's broomstick, taking them
'anywhere, anywhere out of the world', they are often puzzled
to know what writer to turn to; a vague distress of mind making
them unusually fastidious about that sort of intimacy serious
literature establishes between author and reader.

Walt Whitman has written war poems. He, too, lived
through a tense which reeled beneath him. The way he took
those experiences shows a greatness of heart which is very rare,
and yet the feelings he expresses are natural to everybody. He
cannot help us to think more clearly about war, or see things in
a clearer perspective; but he can make us feel more intensely
and in a better way. His war poems are unique because there
is never anything in them which jars with other moods than
the one in which he is considering things. Many poets have
written rattling battle-songs and poems about the tragedies of
war, but almost invariably there is something likely to be even
detestable to a reader who is not in precisely the same mood as
the poet. 'The Battle of the Baltic', for example, is a fine,
spirited war poem, but it may easily seem intolerably trivial
and unreal reading today. But there is a quality in Walt
Whitman's tenderness which harmonises even with the mood
in which the mind contemplates what is exhilarating in a
fighting life, and yet, conversely in his enjoyment of a soldier's
life, there is something not repulsive to those who are conscious
before everything else of the horrors, waste and agonies of war.

Whitman set out to express in literature the average man
through life, and here also he is the average man for he feels
about war both like a pacifist and like a soldier. It may not be
consistent; but the companionship of such a man is comforting

when he has the power to ennoble those contradictory emotions —without seeming to wrong either of them.

Again, there is another quality in his writings which I do not know where to find elsewhere, a quality more difficult to define. It springs from the same emotion which made him the most genuine of democrats. Tragedy usually singles out the individual. The suffering or courage of masses of men is unreal to most of us compared with that of individuals. In Whitman there is no such partiality, and in reading him one never forgets the gigantic scale on which things happen. It's easy enough to take this in as a fact and assent to it intellectually, but it's difficult to apprehend it emotionally, and very difficult then to feel about it like a poet. For, when the imagination is fixed upon the individual he seems all important while the fate of vast numbers becomes only a background to his suffering or endurance; or if it is the whole we think about, then we are inclined to feel, what is one among so many? And we lose sensitiveness. But it is Walt Whitman's special gift to make the individual seem precious while reminding us he is one of a million equals.

Lastly, though, like the ordinary man, he takes a side passionately and never swerves in his conviction that victory was worth while, yet he expresses, too, a mood in which he does not feel himself divided even from those who fought against him, and this he expressed beautifully.

He collected his poems, or chants, called *Leaves of Grass* and in it he says somewhere that he who reads it touches not a book but a man. That is true.

> Behold I do not give lectures or a little charity—
> When I give, I give myself.

He says the same thing repeatedly in different ways—and it is true. Consequently if Whitman means anything at all to you he may mean a great deal. You will cease, then, to care how fine a poet he is, saying to yourself: 'This man may or may not be one of the greater poets, but he gives me an outlook upon the world I value, and though he's dead and shadow, he comes closer to me than many a friend.' On the other hand, if he does not have that effect on you, his work affords ample opportunities for literary debate. Fragments of it—some of his pieces —are undoubtedly of a grand beauty, but pages and pages have hardly any poetic merit at all. Often his poetry is accurately described in his own words:

I sound my barbaric yawp over the roofs of the world.

How soon what is over is forgotten, and the waves wash the imprints off the sand—but I recall that Walt Whitman was to me the best companion of my worst days.

I should like to quote part of a letter he wrote from a military hospital during the American Civil War to a mother, unknown to him, whose son died there. It shows Walt's character.

You will find it in Stevenson's essay on Walt Whitman (*Men and Books*). This is what he wrote:

Frank, as far as I saw, had everything requisite in surgical treatment, nursing, etc. He had watches much of the time. He was so good and well-behaved and affectionate, I myself liked him very much. I was in the habit of coming in afternoons and sitting by him, and he liked to have me—liked to put out his arm and lay his hand on my knee—and would keep it so a long while.

He was perfectly willing to die—he had become very weak, and had suffer'd a good deal, and was perfectly resign'd, poor boy. I do not know his past life, but I feel as if it must have been good. At any rate what I saw of him here, under the most trying circumstances, with a painful wound, and among strangers! I can say that he behaved so brave, so composed, and so sweet and affectionate, it could not be surpassed. And now, like many other noble and good men, after serving his country as a soldier, he has yielded up his young life at the very outset in her service. Such things are gloomy—yet there is a text 'God doeth all things well', the meaning of which, after due time, appears to the soul.

I thought perhaps a few words, though from a stranger, about your son, from one who was with him at the last, might be worth while, for I loved the young man, though I but saw him immediately to lose him.

That is the letter of a good man; one who is not seeking to make a hero out of an ordinary young man, but feels towards him as if no hero could be greater. Walt knew what the mother wanted to hear about Frank; and he told her about Frank as he was.

LAST WORDS ON WELLS

1946

DURING the last year of his long illness I re-read a good many of his books, chiefly books that he wrote before the end of the 1914-18 war. It was a way of keeping in touch with him—a better way than a few minutes' talk with a very tired old man—as tired as a sick child. I re-read quite a number of his romances, his scientific fantasias, *The First Men in the Moon*, some of the most delightful of his short stories, and *The Invisible Man*. I re-read some of his novels—not *Kipps* or *Mr Polly* (two of his best), those I know too well—but *Ann Veronica*, *The New Machiavelli*, *Love and Mr Lewisham* and the more recent (1938) *Apropos of Dolores*. I admired and enjoyed them very much. His imagination was so original and daring; his realism so astonishingly true and so amusing: his phrases and sentences so exact—and frequently beautiful. The novels were 'alive and kicking' as Henry James used to say of them in his letters to Wells, while deploring the author's neglect of form. Oh what an artist spoilt! That was Henry James's refrain in those letters. I re-read, too, some of the many books he wrote about politics, history, science, and Progress—with a capital P. Or rather I read *in* them. I went back to some of the quite early ones, to *A Modern Utopia*, which I remember had made me exclaim in my youth, 'There's truth at the bottom of that Wells.' And among those books was the one which he wrote in 1933, *The Shape of Things to Come*. That I read, though I could not enjoy it, in order to understand how he was suffering today. For (I knew it from pronouncements which were appearing in the Press) he was no longer giving the same answer about things to come as he had given then. Was it because the fire of life was sinking in him? Or was it because he now saw that faith in Progress was only a 'faith', like other faiths his intellect had rejected?

But in 1933 he was the happy possessor of a faith that, in the end, mankind cannot fail to solve the problem of how to live upon this planet.

In seven years, he wrote, Europe was to stumble into another great war, and that would lead 'into a squalor of political fiascoes, unpayable debts, unsubscribed loans, scrapped machinery, insurrection, guerrilla and bandit conflicts, universal hunger and the great pestilences. Gas-warfare and air-warfare fade out of the foreground of human experience, dwarfed and overwhelmed by the more primitive realities of panic, famine and fever.' Half the human race would perish. But *he* was convinced that then, after an age of tyranny necessary to recovery, and compared with which the tyrannies of Sovietism and Hitlerism were mild, mankind, purged at last of folly, and the struggle for material existence over, would then enter into the freedom of a Great World State, scientifically controlled. Mankind would possess its soul in a peace which passes our understanding. And of that book when it came out, I wrote:

Ah! There's the rub! The far-off end fails to console, partly because to us it can't be vividly real, partly because human beings, even when they do care for the good of mankind, care still more— inevitably—for their private good and that of those nearest them. . . . We can care, and really care, for the future of mankind while we are fairly happy ourselves, but when suffering comes to *us*—well, doesn't even a toothache or a threat of insolvency wipe out our interest in world-progress? That is the fact which modern prophets, like Wells and Shaw, who want to base Religion on the conception of Progress, blink.

Yet how right even about dates he was as a prophet in 1933! True, we have survived the disaster of 1940, but what is ahead?

No writer contributed more to the moral and intellectual make-up of the average early twentieth-century man and woman. Maybe they are not today fully conscious of it; for when ideas are, as the phrase goes, 'in the air', they cease to be attributed to any particular person.

The first thing to recall is that he was a writer of genius who was obsessed by the problems of his time, the second that he was the first really gifted writer (Jules Verne is too boyish to count in this connection) whose imagination in a scientific age was saturated with scientific ideas. In early days (and intermittently afterwards) he played delightfully and amusingly with them. Indeed so entertainingly that from time to time people would say that his early short stories were his best contributions to literature. That was absurd.

Until the idea of Progress—it was born in the eighteenth century—got hold of men's minds, writers placed Utopias in the past. Their imaginations dwelt on the happy and 'noble savage', not on a happy and splendid man to be. With command over nature came the conception of Progress, and the idea of an Eden ahead, not behind. No writer has believed more passionately and persistently in the future of mankind than Wells. It is hardly necessary to recall how many Utopias or 'anticipations' are to be found among his many books. These in varying degrees show two characteristics: they are based upon the faith that it is through applied science such dreams can be made realities; and secondly, in most, the political steps to be immediately taken are also suggested.

But if the 'prophet' in Wells, the reformer and imaginative man of science, had not also been combined with a born novelist, his influence over so many in all countries would never have been so great. His strength as a novelist lay in his being himself in many respects an average man—a fact which hid from some who knew him his greater side. He cared persistently, excitedly—even pathetically—for the creation of a better civilisation. It was the driving power behind his huge, unceasing, miscellaneous output. On that passion alone he prided himself. In many other directions in his work and his life, he often exhibited an almost slovenly humility and carelessness. Because he was ordinary, he knew where the shoe of contemporary civilisation pinched the average chaotic nonentity today, preventing him or her from walking surefootedly. Yet he felt the value and believed in the reasonableness of hope. He trusted the generous impulses of adolescence, however ignorant, preposterous, and easily extinguished, and he appealed to the young. No one understood better, too, their ridiculous amorous predicaments (had he not shared them?).

He was obsessed by himself and by the problems of his own times, but the history of Literature shows that this is frequently the way to interest other men and other times. But a natural impetuosity, encouraged, I believe, by his theory of the artist's function (Literature is the Soul of the World doing its own thinking), often prevented his making any particular book as good as he could have made it. As long as this thought or that emotion impinged somehow on someone, he did not care about bringing its expression to greater perfection. Once in a phrase, apparently modest, but concealing an enormous claim, he compared the writer to a telegraph boy who delivers a message— of course from on high. He was in consequence contemptuously impatient of the novelists who thought their work their own affair, and held that form was important (Henry James and George Moore, for example). His method of constructing a book was often just to take the back out of the cart of his mind, tilt up the shafts and let the contents fall with an exhilarating rumble. And the most important part of his 'message' has been to persuade us that civilisation is malleable and easily altered. In youth, taking the clue from our own natures, which at that time of life seem easily alterable for the better, we are ready to believe that the same is true of the world. For at every period of life we judge not only other people but the world by ourselves. When our passions die down we see the foolish and vain side of passion, and when our life cools we cease to believe that enthusiasm and energy are sufficient to change fundamentally our environment. But which is right—youth or age? Wells, until the end of his life, thought youth was right.

SIEGFRIED SASSOON

1946

IT WAS a piece of good fortune as far as Siegfried Sassoon's personal fame is concerned, that it was the war of 1914 which turned him into a poet. It has increased the chance of his proving of interest to posterity, even at some date when perhaps better poets may be surviving, quasi-anonymously, only in an anthologised specimen or two of their work. It was also fortunate for the world that the young man whom that war made into a poet should have been a wayward, impulsive being, imperfectly unified.

On the one hand, he was typical of that generation who volunteered to serve in a spirit which was half joy of life and half readiness to die; on the other, he was representative of the pacifists, intellectual or emotional, who, as the slaughter mounted year after year, became more deeply convinced that war was a filthy, useless business, from which no good could possibly come, and had its roots in the cold-blooded idiocy of diplomacy and in vested interests bawling patriotically and making money.

Examine himself as he might, and he was an honest young man, he could not be sure for very long together if he were most genuinely himself when he felt and spoke like the 'Old Sig' who loved hunting and games and the spontaneous idea-less companionship of faithful cronies, who half-liked, in spite of everything, life at the front and enjoyed danger, too, when that was a matter of taking active personal risks; or when he was the reflective, sensitive, musical, literary Siegfried Sassoon, on whom the responsibility of being able to look at things with detachment either weighed like a stone or acted like a sudden spur. His reading of himself seemed to depend on the kind of company he was keeping. And, with sympathetic natures in need of sympathy themselves, that must often be so; general ideas, political convictions do not seem to such men as intensely real as personal relations. They are not made for causes which arbitrarily divide their fellow-men into enemies and friends. When he was at the front his mind at any rate was at peace; with comrades by his side he could not be 'above the combat'. But on sick-leave as a wounded hero he was at war with himself.

It is not easy for those who have known only this war to understand that emotional conflict. In this war it was clear all along that it had to be fought to a finish; secondly, pacifist ideology could not be applied with the same plausibility to its origin; and, finally, the fact that civilians had to share to a large extent the dangers, and saw and felt the horrors, of war, purified the expression of patriotic emotion at home. The 'talkers' in the last war were often intolerable, and the Press was sometimes nearly as bad. In this war I did not hear of a fighting man on leave preferring the company of a pacifist, but in the last, after 1916, men in the Services who dodged as far as possible their war-fervid friends and relatives were not uncommon.

The young Siegfried Sassoon resolved that those at home who revelled in glorifying life at the front, whether from thick-skinned lack of imagination or from a sense of duty in keeping up morale, should at any rate be made to look also at some of its ugly realities. The result was that series of bitter war-poems which shocked the conventional and the romantic, infuriated those who loved to fight with their tongues, and delighted the pacifists—poems which have been remembered.

What followed he has described in two sections of his more or less alembicised autobiography (one of the most remarkable books of its kind), *The Complete Memoirs of George Sherston*, namely, 'The Memoirs of an Infantry Officer' and 'Sherston's Progress'. In *Siegfried's Journey* he goes over those years again in more detail. He covers the years when he made up his mind that it was his duty to take advantage of the fact that he was both a successful poet and a wounded war-hero with the Military Cross, to help the stop-the-war movement. The response of the War Office to his declaration that when passed as fit again for service he would refuse to obey orders, was to send him to a military hospital for shell-shock cases near Edinburgh.

In *Siegfried's Journey* we hear more about the psychologist, Rivers, in whose charge he was placed and who helped him so much; about Wilfred Owen, who became his friend and, as a poet, learnt from him; and about that inner conflict which finally led him willy-nilly to go back to the front as a soldier. It is very interesting indeed. *Sherston's Progress*, from a literary point of view, was even more remarkable. The interests and merits of *Siegfried's Journey* live in the admirable portraits of well-known people he met, the description of his feelings (mixed) on finding himself 'lionised' as a poet or as a heroic-pacifist, his accounts of his post-war political support of Snowden, of his work as a literary editor, and of his lecturing-crusade as a Man of Peace in America. But running all through these stories is a dawning discovery that he was never really meant to be a servant of Causes, but a ruminator on life.

There is a passage in *Sherston's Progress* worth quoting in this connection which runs:

My main difficulty has been that I absorb so much that I am continually asking to be allowed to sit still and digest the good (and bad) things which life has offered me.

A ruminator really needs two lives; one for experiencing and another for thinking it over. Knowing that I *need* two lives and am allowed one, I do my best to *lead* two lives; with the inevitable consequence that I am told by the world's busybodies that I am 'turning my back on the contemporary situation'. Such people are usually so busy trying to crowd the whole of life into their daily existence that they get very little of it permanently inside their craniums. My own idea is that it is better to carry the best part of one's life about in one's head for future reference.

The instinct which has led him to project now in verse, now in admirable prose, his past experience, has been a sure one.

At first it may seem strange that a poet should have spent so large a part of his life in writing autobiography. He has gone over as a memoirist the same ground, though, of course, with fresh detail, which he had covered in *Memoirs of a Fox-hunting Man* and the Sherston series. *The Weald of Youth, The Old Century*, and now *Siegfried's Journey* together cover his life from childhood to 1920. But it has been well worth while. For apart from that literary skill and fineness of observation which give intense pleasure to readers, his temperament and adventures have enabled him to help us to understand our own times.

LOGAN PEARSALL SMITH

1946

LOGAN PEARSALL SMITH died a week ago in his house in Chelsea, at the age of eighty. On 1st January he had sent me a copy of *All Trivia* (Constable), which includes 'Trivia' (1902), 'More Trivia' (1922), 'Afterthoughts' (1931) and 'Last Words' (1933). *All Trivia* has been reprinted four times, parts of it have been translated into several languages, and it has found a surprising number of readers in America and in France. Once when we were in Paris together he bought a copy of the French translation of the first two 'Trivias', among other books, and when the bookseller inquired how the parcel should be directed, I remember the reverence with which he asked, '*Monsieur, êtes-vous le grand Monsieur Smit?*' As we left the shop my old friend said, 'Pity, things always come too late. What pleasure that would have given me when I was young!' Nevertheless he did enjoy, intermittently, his ever-growing reputation during his last years. He was vain, but self-consciously vain, and with a spice of irony; and the triumph he felt when he perceived that he had expressed himself perfectly meant far more to him than praise.

But his growing fame was also welcome as confirming what he had preached incessantly, that style is the sole preservative. Of course, it must be suited to the matter in hand, and his own prose exhibits varying degrees of elaboration in *The Life of Wotton*, his critical essays and *Unforgotten Years*. Yet each is written with equal care. The last book belongs to the class of autobiographies at the head of which stands Gibbon's *Memoirs*. And it comes high in the list. It is written with pleasing smoothness and ironic detachment. It resembles the great historian's little masterpiece of retrospection in being the story of a vocation. Alas, it stops when he is in his early thirties, when, after Oxford and a sojourn in Paris, he settled in an old Sussex farm (rent and garden £30) to learn and practise the lovely art of writing.

Among the early chapters describing his Quaker surroundings, his religious parents, his childhood, boyhood and youth in America, and his escape from the family business, there is also one which brings old Walt Whitman vividly to life. Of *Leaves of Grass* he wrote:

> It gave us ears, it gave us eyes, it revealed to us the miracle of our own existence, and for me, at least, with my meagre ideals of borrowed culture, it seemed to open a great shining window in my narrow house of life.

Unforgotten Years is an autobiography with a lesson, which is also a cheering one. Its moral is that if only we care genuinely enough about the art of writing we can acquire it without possessing genius. 'The test of a vocation is the love of the drudgery it involves.'

Yet anything less like *Leaves of Grass* than the contribution to literature he was destined to make himself, is hard to imagine. One of the later trivia runs thus:

> When by sips of champagne and a few oysters they can no longer keep me from fading away into the infinite azure, 'You cannot', I shall whisper my last faint message to the world, 'be too fastidious.'

His death is so recent that to me that is a moving valediction. It does express, and with a consciousness of extravagance most characteristic, his ruling passion as a man of letters. And here is an earlier tell-tale passage. Listen to the undertone of irony:

> 'Occult, night-wandering, enormous, honey-pale—or blanc, as Milton calls her—' The morning paper lay there unopened; I knew I ought to look at the news, for the crash was awful, but I was too busy just then trying to find an adjective for the Moon—the magical, mooney epithet, which could I only find or invent, what then would matter the quakes and sublunary conflicts of this negligible earth?

Trivia (1902), that tiny volume, was the fruit of Sussex retirement. It met with no appreciation—unless the respect

of Robert Bridges, mingled, however, with severe moral dis-
approval, can be counted as such. In most of his friends, and
hardly a copy travelled beyond them, *Trivia* aroused only
angry contempt. There are readers, and good readers, too, to
whom a self-delighting, self-conscious preciosity is irritating.
In verse they may tolerate it—they often have to—but in
prose they cannot get away with it. A sense of proportion,
more ethical than aesthetic, stands between them and what
they might otherwise enjoy. Although it was clear that no
writer could have been more aware than he of the extravagance,
in a world bursting with misery, of his own passion for words
and their nice arrangement, that awareness by no means
propitiated them. Indeed, they were the more exasperated by
it. Pater, with his sanctuary style, was bad enough, but at
least he wrote consistently as an other-worldly aesthete. But
here a similar, careful elaboration was lavished also on recording
the oddities of existence and often petty, if amusing, social and
private embarrassments. They did not see that it was there the
value and originality of *Trivia* lay.

Walter Pater was the most pervasive influence during the
first half of his literary life, and of him he has written beautifully
in *Reperusals and Recollections*. Later, it was in the works of
Santayana that he found the best expression of that philosophic
aesthetic detachment which appealed so deeply to him. Of all
his anthologies he was most proud of his selection of passages
from Santayana's works, *Little Essays* (Constable). I hope some
time to draw his portrait, difficult though it be to do so, for I
owe him much and posterity will be interested in him. As I
have said before, I believe *Trivia* is the sort of bibelot that
Father Time often keeps on his mantelpiece when he turns out
the big furniture in his house; the beds in which many have
slept, the wardrobes in which they have hung their ideas. And,
apart from *Trivia*, if taste for good criticism survives, the best
essays of Pearsall Smith—for example his preface to *English
Aphorisms*—will continue to be read. Meanwhile let me try to
find, as he would, a formula for his specific contribution.

His most original work strikes me as proceeding from a man with an ineradicable sense of moral responsibilities and a craving for social pleasures, who would fain have lived only for thrills of aesthetic exaltation, 'those suggestions of an ideal world which we feel in the presence of any true beauty'. One who had found that the Ivory Tower is liable to irruptions, sometimes from the outside world, sometimes from within himself. Often these were comic, sometimes painfully humiliating. Life might be a continual warning to live only in the imagination, but it wasn't possible to take it. So he set himself to record honestly and with exquisite skill not only the adventures of his poetic sensibility, but all the odd turns of his emotions and grotesque movements of his mind.

The sudden pricking of the iridescent bubble of dreams and vanities, encased in which we move through life, was one of his favourite themes. Thus this mandarin of the art of letters incidentally became a moralist, this devotee of detachment an ironist of the contemplative life. He observed others with all the excited interest of a gossip, but he brought to our tea-tables and dinner-tables something of the solitude of the thinker. The results were often fascinating. 'How awful to reflect'—so runs one of his aphorisms—'that what people say of us is true! How incredible, too, that this being I call "myself" who at moments seems even able to embrace the Universe, and comprehends his fellow-creatures so condescendingly, should nevertheless be to them only a commonplace creature, limited and quite easy to describe!'

He remained true to his own ruling passion. In a world full of vain pursuits, which also attracted him, he preserved in safety his own not ignoble 'vanity'—his pet fanaticism: 'What above all things I should like would be to make out of life—how shall I put it?—something delicate and durable. . . . To live on, in fact, after my funeral in a perfect phrase.' I think he will.

TENNYSON

1946

MR AUDEN'S selection from Tennyson is the first in a series of anthologies to be called *The Poets on Poets*; several other volumes are in preparation. It contains many of Tennyson's best and most renowned short poems, and yet it strikes me, on the whole, as a rather casual, indolent selection. Moreover, the tone of the Introduction is very patronising. It reads as if Mr Auden had been feeling while he wrote it like a middle-aged schoolmaster preparing a report on little Alfred's work and general behaviour. This may irritate some of his readers, yet presently they may also smile—it has a comic aspect.

The anthology runs to 300 pages. Of these 'In Memoriam' and 'Maud' occupy together 117. Considering how much space was needed for other good poems it was probably a mistake to reprint 'In Memoriam' in full. That poem is divided, as Tennyson said in one of its stanzas, into 'short swallow-flights of song', and these are by no means all of equal beauty or depth, and are easily separable. Not a few might therefore have been omitted to make room for poems of greater merit, such as 'Flow down cold rivulet to the sea'; 'Early Spring', which begins

> Once more the Heavenly Power
> Makes all things new;

'God and the Universe', which concentrates into two stanzas the mysteries over which the poet brooded all his life; and the 'Invitation to F. D. Maurice'. The list might be made longer. As for the dramatic-monologue, 'Maud', which is not nearly as long, Mr Auden was probably right to abstain from cutting that pathological soliloquy of 'a brainless Hamlet'—so Oliver Elton called the hero—a figure on no account to be identified

149

with the poet himself, although he is a projection of moods (as other poems prove) which Tennyson knew well. The marvel of 'Maud' is the psychologically dramatic truth of its splendid rhetoric, and also the frequency with which phrases and passages in it through their sound summon things before the imagination, while at the same time presenting us with pictures consummately concise.

As every anthologist of a famous poet knows—and any reader might guess as much—his most difficult discriminations begin after he has exhausted the acknowledged masterpieces and comes to choosing the best among the nearly best, and when he has to make up his mind whether or not he will include passages, as good as the poet's best poems, taken from poems not nearly so good as wholes. Such passages abound in Tennyson; and I much regret that Mr Auden confined himself to quoting poems in their entirety. The one exception is 'The Vision of Sin'—unless you count the omission of some lines from 'Locksley Hall'. This decision has diminished the richness of his anthology. For instance, instead of the pretty, but merely pretty, 'Roses on the Terrace', he might have taken from 'The Ancient Sage' (it would not have needed more space) that lyric:

> O rose tree planted in my grief,
>   And growing on her tomb,
> Her dust is greening in your leaf,
>   Her blood is in your bloom.

And how Mr Auden could have included that poor sentimentally sensational story 'Despair', instead of such an expression of the poet's own despair as 'Vastness', I cannot understand:

> Raving politics, never at rest—as this
> Poor earth's pale history runs—
> What is it all but the trouble of ants in the
> Gleam of a million million of suns
>
> .   .   .   .
>
> What the philosophies, all the sciences,
> Poesy, varying voices of prayer?

All that is noblest, all that is basest, all
That is filthy with all that is fair?

What is it all, if we all of us end
But in being our own corpse-coffins at last,
Swallowed in Vastness, lost in Silence,
Drowned in the deeps of a meaningless past?

'Vastness' has power at any rate, while 'Despair' might have been the work of G. R. Sims.

Any Tennyson anthology to be valuable must include many extracts; he was so sublimely, so shockingly uneven. Not otherwise will a young reader who comes to him fresh, or with prejudice, appreciate to the full the lovely dexterities of this 'landscape-lover, lord of Language', in whose most faulty poems may be found

All the charm of all the Muses
Often flowering in a lonely word.

Whatever the defects of the decorative-heroic style of 'The Idylls of the King', or of its story-telling or (obvious to any modern reader) of its scolding treatment of passionate love, the reader cannot turn those pages without finding such absolute felicities as, say, the description of Merlin's forebodings:

So dark a forethought rolled about his brain
As on a dull day in an ocean cave
The blind wave feeling round his long sea-hole
In silence.

Or such a simile for petty, lasting resentment as this:

But ever after, the small violence done
Rankled in him and ruffled all his heart,
As the sharp wind that ruffles all day long
A little bitter pool about a stone
On the bare coast.

Or this for Guinevere's 'vague spiritual fear':

Like to some doubtful noise of creaking doors,
Heard by the watcher in a haunted house,
That keeps the rust of murder on the walls . . .

In that book, 'Guinevere', there occurs, by the by, one of the rare real moments of passion in all 'The Idylls of the King', when she and Lancelot

> Hands in hands and eye to eye
> Low on the border of her couch they sat
> Stammering and staring. It was their last hour,
> A madness of farewells.

'A madness of farewells'—what a magnificent phrase!

One cannot read even one of his Victorian novelettes like *Aylmer's Field* without stumbling upon some sudden glory:

> Lay hidden as the music of the moon
> Sleeps in the plain eggs of the nightingale.

How admirably precise his pen is, too, when he dips it in contempt:

> Slight Sir Robert with his watery smile
> And educated whisker.

No one would include, today, 'The Gardener's Daughter' in a Selected Tennyson, yet what English pictures it contains!

> Not wholly in the busy world, nor quite
> Beyond it blooms the garden that I love.
> News from the humming city comes to it
> In sound of funeral or of marriage bells;
> And sitting muffled in dark leaves, you hear
> The windy clanging of the minster clock;
> Although between it and the garden lies
> A league of grass, wash'd by a slow broad stream,
> That, stirr'd with languid pulses of the oar,
> Waves all its lazy lilies and creeps on,
> Barge-laden, to three arches of a bridge
> Crown'd with the minster-towers.

And I cannot forbear adding one more line from it:

> From the woods
> Came voices of the well-contented doves.

If that compound adjective gives you a small thrill of pleasure you are a potential Tennysonian. It is one of his average not supreme felicities, and therefore a test. Of course there are finer examples of his pencraft in far finer poems, many of which are included in this anthology, but if you pass that test (I am addressing some reader who has hardly glanced at Tennyson), it will be worth while to buy instead the collected works—just as cheap; such things are scattered up and down them.

The following passage will indicate the tone of Mr Auden's selection. After giving a concise account of his birth and education, and after mentioning what he calls his 'curious journey with Hallam to the Pyrenees to take money from English sympathisers to a Spanish revolutionary general' he proceeds to summarise Tennyson's life after the death of Hallam, in 1830, thus:

For the next ten years he published no book, had no regular occupation, drank port, smoked strong tobacco, and was poor and unhappy. He became engaged to his future wife; the engagement was broken off.... He invested his capital and his mother's [he did not, but some of his brothers invested some of their money] in the project of a certain Dr Allen for making wood-carving by machinery; the project failed. But at this time he was writing, and in 1842 *Poems* appeared, which established his reputation with the intelligentsia and the critics. In 1846 the grant of a pension from the Civil List made him financially secure [*it was £200 a year*], and in 1850 he published 'In Memoriam', married, and succeeded Wordsworth as Poet Laureate. From then on he led the life of a famous author. He bought a house in the Isle of Wight, he wrote, he grew a beard, he visited Queen Victoria at Osborne, he built another house in Surrey, he went on writing, he visited the Queen at Windsor, he was gazetted to the Peerage, he still wrote. On October 8, 1892, he died, and was buried in Westminster Abbey.

Note the censorious superiority of the tone: for ten years after 1830 Tennyson smokes, drinks, produces nothing, then grows rich and 'a beard' and 'writes', visits the Queen and goes 'on writing', becomes a peer and 'still writes on'. No one would infer from this that Tennyson had written anything to be called poetry after he had settled at Faringford. And this impression is reinforced by the paragraph which immediately follows:

In youth he looked like a gypsy; in age like a dirty old monk; he had the finest ear, perhaps, of any English poet; he was undoubtedly the stupidest; there was little about melancholia that he didn't know; there was little else that he did.

Poor, congenitally morbid, empty-headed arrivist who sold his early poetic gift for riches and success! How different from some poets and authors today, leaders of the young, champions of the oppressed, beacons of the future, thinkers, who, when civilisation and their fellow-countrymen were in danger, promptly left for Hollywood!... It is a mistake, however, to lose one's temper with nonsense, it is better to expose it.

But where begin when it is so tightly packed? Well, let's start with the years following Hallam's death, during which (one hears the reproving voice) Tennyson had no regular occupation, drank port, smoked strong tobacco and was poor and unhappy. Yes, those years were unhappy, most of them, yet they were the most fruitful in his life. He wrote then those numerous Elegies which became 'In Memoriam', also 'The Two Voices', that colloquy with his despair; also 'Ulysses', soon after Hallam's death. It expressed, he has told us, 'my feeling about the need of going forward and braving the struggle of life perhaps more simply than anything in "In Memoriam".' Mr Auden's comment on 'Ulysses' is that it is 'a covert refusal to be a responsible and useful person'. It was during those years Tennyson wrote the lyric, 'O, that t'were possible after long grief and pain', out of which 'Maud' grew, 'Maud', which magnifies some of his own tormented moods during the years of his broken engagement. Part of 'The Princess', too, was written in Lincoln's Inn Fields, though not published till much later.

It is naïve of Mr Auden—or is he generalising from his experience of poets that they instantly publish what they have written?—to suppose ignorantly that the years between 1830 and 1840 must have been lazy and barren. Tennyson said of himself that he did not become an artist till he was nearly thirty, although earlier his genius sometimes carried him through. It may be difficult for a poet like Mr Auden, whose fine effects rest on the animation of spoken words and spoken syntax, to realise that other poems have often required long incubation, but as a critic he should have recalled that that decade produced, in part or complete, a large proportion of the poems he has chosen as the best.

As for the statement that Tennyson was undoubtedly 'the stupidest of English poets', and knew little about anything except melancholia, it is difficult to tell if its source is ignorance or arrogance—probably both.

If there is one fact certain about Tennyson the man, it is that his eminent contemporaries, whatever their attitude towards life—whether they were philosophers like Mill and Sidgwick, men of science like Huxley, Lubbock, Herschel, Catholic thinkers like Wilfred Ward, broad-churchmen like Frederick Maurice, scholars like Jowett, Mark Pattison and Spedding, theists like Martineau, historians like Froude, critics like Leslie Stephen, Hutton and Bagehot, orthodox Christians like Gladstone, Dean Stanley, Archbishop Trench—one and all agreed in their respect for his mind. 'The Metaphysical Society' which included most of the above names, would not have elected 'the stupidest of English poets' as their first president. What struck Huxley in Tennyson was his insight into scientific method, and what impressed the sceptical Sidgwick was that while Wordsworth's attitude towards nature had left science unregarded, in Tennyson the physical world was always that known to us through physical science. He had expressed 'the indestructible and inalienable minimum of faith which humanity cannot give up' and also the force of intellectual doubt. Of course Mr Auden could not have been unaware of how Tennyson appeared in eyes of his contemporaries, though with that crippling arrogance with which others of his generation have had to contend, he probably dismissed such evidence as the worthless testimony of a lot of Victorian bourgeois intellectuals. Still, I wonder what he makes of Carlyle's description of Tennyson's talk as 'speech and speculation free and plentious;

I do not meet in these later decades such company over a pipe';
or of Fitzgerald's confession that he had felt 'a sense of depression at times from the overshadowing of a so much more lofty
intellect than my own'. Carlyle was not a lenient judge of his
contemporaries. He once described Mill's mind as 'sawdust
up to the mast head' and Ruskin's as 'a beautiful bottle of soda
water'; nor was Fitzgerald a fool. Such tributes are difficult to
reconcile with a verdict that Tennyson 'was undoubtedly the
stupidest of English poets' and knew little else but his own
melancholy moods. Mr Auden may have also forgotten that
'In Memoriam' appeared nine years before *The Origin of
Species*. 'Tennyson', as Romanes wrote in *Darwin and After
Darwin*, 'noted the fact (Natural Selection) and a few years
later Darwin supplied the explanation'. Mr Auden may have
thought that such stanzas as

> Are God and Nature then at strife,
>   That Nature sends such evil dreams?
>   So careful of the type she seems,
> So careless of the single life.

were versified impressions taken from Darwin.

When Tennyson, confronted with the mystery of the Universe, compares himself to

> An infant crying in the night;
> An infant crying for the light;
> And with no language but a cry;

Mr Auden calls this an 'extraordinarily acute' self-diagnosis,
and reaches his definition of Tennyson as 'the great English poet
of the Nursery'. Newton once compared himself to a child
picking up pebbles on the shore of the infinite ocean. Perhaps
some day Mr Auden will sum Newton up as the great English
scientist of the schoolroom.

THURBER AND LEAR

1951

Thurber, the humorist, is as hard to expound as a lyric poet, and what a failure critics sometimes make of doing that cannot have escaped your notice—especially if they start from some theory about Poetry itself, or grind an axe with which to lop lofty overshadowing reputations, in the hope of more sunlight reaching their own little sapling. I may not be able to reveal adequately the nature of Thurber's merits, but at least I have no theory about the nature of true humour to hamper me in appreciating him. I distrust all theories about Humour for the same reasons that I distrust theories about Poetry. I have read, or read about, far too many of the latter not to have perceived that none have lasted and that most of them contradict each other. While each theory has claimed to be of universal application, it has been clear to me that if any one of them had been generally accepted as authoritative, the world would have lost a quite gigantic amount of good poetry.

Although short-lived aesthetic theories can, of course, do damage (the visual arts today seem to be writhing rather helplessly in their embraces), yet theories can also serve a useful purpose, sometimes by suggesting to an individual poet something really worth trying, sometimes by drawing the attention of critics and readers to qualities in some work or other which might otherwise have escaped their notice. Theories wither when accepted as dogmas, but they may be helpful as hints.

There have not been nearly as many answers to the question What is Humour? as to What is Poetry? Still, there have been plenty of them, and most come under two main heads: (1) That what amuses is what makes us feel superior, laughter being really always at the expense of someone or something. And that (2) laughter is always the result of a sudden release from social and moral inhibitions, which explains why sex is the source of so many jokes, and why disrespectful flippancy or outrageous understatement are often funny.

Hobbes was the founder of school No. 1. I remember that when I first heard his definition, 'Laughter is a sudden glory', I took it for a splendid phrase descriptive of laughter itself. When I discovered that he meant that being amused was always the same as a sense of triumphant superiority, I thought him crass. Yet this superiority theory has by no means died out; you will find it in various forms and degrees in modern thinkers. Freud and other psychologists are, of course, exponents of the inhibition theory of Humour. But neither of these theories work, in spite of the ingenuity with which they have been applied; they do not cover the ground, but only patches of it. They do not explain Thurber, for example.

Without attempting to define humour, I should like to say this about its function: it is one way of coming to terms with what is painful or humiliating. As Mark Twain and others have remarked, there will be no jokes in heaven. Indeed, humorists have often been somewhat melancholy—Molière, Cervantes, Mark Twain. 'If we cannot get the better of life', I once wrote, 'at any rate we can be so free as to laugh at it: if we cannot help being insignificant, we can at any rate acknowledge the fact gracefully with a joke, thereby keeping in touch with a larger sense of things.' Humour is not a mere distraction, it is a consolation; it is a way of honestly facing facts without being overwhelmed by them.

Take, for example, the amusing drawings in Thurber's *The Last Flower* series, which reflect in pictures mankind's history after a Twelfth World War. It is *da capo* panorama, the same beginnings, the same consequences, the same scenes of slow recovery and of sudden destruction—until, finally, only one lonely small broken flower is left upon the earth. What could be more dismal? Granted: yet there *is* a morsel of greatness in silly little men—even that can make them laugh. And note that

men and women in these pictures, as indeed in most incidents
Thurber has recorded, are, whether they be odious or merely
stupid, people to whom—although they may be sometimes
depicted as smiling—no one would ever dream of attributing
a grain of humour. This often makes their predicaments quite
enormously comic. This also is an ingredient in his delightful
'Fables' of the Crow who left his wife to court an Oriole bird,
the Owl who was God, and the Stork who married a dumb
wife, etc.

There is no doubt in my mind that America's greatest contribution to imaginative life on this planet has been, so far, a
humorous one. Americans have not only discovered new jokes,
colloquially and pictorially, which have lately influenced the
whole world, but they have added huge regions to the kingdom
of humour.

This comment by Max Eastman is well worth pondering:

It is no accident that Mark Twain and Abraham Lincoln, both
men in whom humour took the place of ideological hankerings—
have remained in the world's eyes representative Americans. Their
headstrong sensibilities, their steadfast confrontation of fact, and
their adjustment through humorous emotion to the predicament in
which facts steadfastly confronted place the wishful heart of man, is
the keynote of our culture if we have one.

Thurber, too, is an offspring of America's national mind,
but that is not the aspect of him I want to stress now.

He certainly had one predecessor—whether he was also his
begetter I do not know—an Englishman, Edward Lear, who,
by the by, had few descendants in this country, and only among
a few illustrators of children's books. What Lear's and Thurber's drawings have in common is that they are in themselves
comic. Up to well into the twentieth century the best humorous
artists, with the exception of some caricaturists, *illustrated*
humour, but did not create it out of lines and forms. Their
skill lay in first visualising, then in depicting, interpreting or
dramatising amusing situations which not only always could be,
but invariably were, also expressed in words—usually in a bit

of dialogue underneath the picture itself. (Gavarni, Leech, Keene, for example.) It was the American draughtsmen, Peter Arno and James Thurber, who revealed to British editors and the British public (via *The New Yorker*) that purely pictorial humour could be enormously enjoyable.

Thurber has recorded in *The Beast in Me and Other Animals* how some of his best pictures grew in his mind during a kind of absent-minded semi-conscious process, not unlike that which sometimes successfully brings a poem to birth. Take that famous picture of a seal at the back of a double-bed, with its caption, 'All right, have it your own way—you heard a seal bark.' You will remember, if you ever saw that drawing, the skill with which an exasperated husband, sick to death of arguing about the utterly impossible, is depicted as turning away from a jawing, arguing wife as he says those words. 'The picture started out to be', Thurber tells us, 'a seal on a rock. The rock in the process of being drawn, began to look like the head of a bed, so I made a bed out of it, put a man and wife in the bed, and stumbled on to the caption as easily and unexpectedly as the seal had stumbled into the bedroom.'

Again, that picture of the woman crouched on the top of a bookcase and a host receiving his astounded guest with the words: 'That's my first wife up there and this is the *present* Mrs Harris,' also grew in the same way. Happy, happy Mr Thurber, whose doodling has been so fruitful!

Unlike Thurber, Edward Lear at the start 'doodled' with words, not shapes; melodious, or as he liked to call them 'meloobious', words bestowed on him the freedom of the City of Nonsense; but once there he could also express in line and form what he found. Of course there must always be a tiny spark of sense in Nonsense or it would not be funny at all. Its fascination largely depends on our feeling it is there without being able to pin it down.

Aldous Huxley identifies those referred to so often as 'they' in Lear's nonsense rhymes, as 'the world', 'public opinion', or 'all right thinking men and women', between whom and the individualist there is eternal war, in which sometimes the one is victorious and sometimes the herd. I think that ideological interpretation fits nicely. There is, of course, far more social criticism in Thurber's pictorial humour; indeed he is often definitely satirical. Both have in common another characteristic proper to imaginative humorists—a perpetual wonder at animal and vegetable life. Both love inventing, drawing and naming animals and plants queer enough to be creations of Nature herself; nor with them does familiarity—as it does with most of us—ever diminish amazed amusement at her invention.

F

PEOPLE

DR WATSON

1929

A T NO other period of literary history have biographers shown such brilliant independence of documents, such ingenuity in surmise. Biographers of an earlier date would never have told us, for instance, that cats were playing in the area, or a milk-cart was passing by when Keats was born, nor did it occur to them to introduce their hero, as it were, *incognito*, a minor figure in the midst of some trivial but brilliantly imagined scene. They, the old biographers, began, you remember, in a different fashion. They opened with a statement of the place and date at which the biographee was born, and with an account of his descent. I cannot bring home to you more directly the drawback of such old-fashioned methods than by saying at once that, if we still adhered to them, it would be almost impossible to write the life of the most representative Englishman of the latter end of the nineteenth century—I mean, of course, Dr Watson, friend and chronicler of Sherlock Holmes.

We do not know precisely the date of his birth, and had not his agitation on hearing a few melancholy facts deduced from his brother's watch betrayed him, we should know little about any single member of his family. Dr Watson, in all things typical of his generation, is in none more unlike our own than in his reluctance to make family skeletons dance in public. Although he has never shown the slightest shyness about being drawn, so that did not his moustache, his clothes and his bowler resemble those of countless other men, we should recognise him in the streets, he has always been exceedingly chary of facts about himself, unless they were pertinent to the 'adventure' in hand. This self-respecting, self-effacing habit proclaims his sound middle-class descent, for, though a proud reserve was once supposed to be a sign of breeding, a flighty and confident exhibitionism has become almost the sole remaining peculiarity of too many aristocrats.

And I may add that both he and his friend also betray that descent in their respectfully romantic, yet self-consciously independent attitude towards people of title. For Dr Watson even a baronet or a coroneted envelope adds to the unenvied glamour of the world. Let me add that here he has my entire sympathy: nothing is so dull as equality; where there is no inequality there is no fun.

Owing to this paucity of direct information, though, as I shall presently suggest, Dr Watson has told us more about himself than he perhaps intended, you will not be surprised to hear that I have elected to open my forthcoming and profusely illustrated biography of him in the modern fashion.

The second Afghan War is on the point of breaking out; the great men of the time pass rapidly across the page, diminished, however, to pigmy size in the perspective of my own powerful and quizzical intellect. At last, upon the crowded deck of a steamer destined for Bombay, the reader is permitted to observe a young straight-backed, strong-backed Army surgeon. He is attached to the Fifth Northumberland Fusiliers, already stationed in India. He has a fair moustache and he is correctly if inexpensively dressed. Although it is his habit to cling to his bowler in roughest parts of rural England he discards it in the Red Sea. His opinions are wholesome and invariably predictable.

This, you perceive, is the new *incognito* method. The reader is gently titillated by his shrewd guess that this young man is no other than *the* Dr Watson, though the young man himself —and I believe this is what the Greeks called irony—is ignorant (not, of course, of the fact), but of its far-flung implications. Though reserved in print there is no reason to suppose that Lieutenant Watson would be otherwise than modestly frank in conversation; and, adopting the modern biographer's privilege of recording conversations which did not take place and embodying in them remarks uttered on other occasions, I shall then have an opportunity of narrating his life up to that date—

without pinning myself down to tiresome particularities. He has told us himself that he took his degree of Doctor of Medicine of the University of London in 1878. Well, from evidence it would take too long to marshal, we know he was not brilliant. Indeed, I have always suspected that when Holmes refused, in *The Case of the Dying Detective*, to allow Watson to prescribe for him and told him roundly that he was 'only a general practitioner with very limited experience and mediocre qualifications', the great man was not only acting a part but also speaking his mind. No: Lieutenant Watson would not be 'our Watson' if he had passed his examinations quickly. He would have taken a full five years and more to qualify. If, then, he entered London University at the average age he would be twenty-four when he took his degree, thus we arrive at the date of his birth, 1854. He arrived in India just in time for the battle of Maiwand, which took place in July, 1880, so when his biographer first catches sight of him and overhears him he is twenty-six. Highly susceptible, as his courtship of Miss Morston in *The Sign of Four* shows, honest caution would lead him, though scrupulously polite, to avoid female companionship on board. It would be, then, in the deck smoking room (minutely described) that he would impart the following facts about himself: that he had only his professional prospects, and 'neither kith nor kin in England'; that his late father had been an unsuccessful man but a conscientious parent who had emigrated to Australia; that his elder brother had been a great cause of anxiety and disappointment; that he himself had spent his childhood in Australia; then been sent to England to a small inexpensive school, where a nephew by marriage of a lord (you remember, of course, 'Tadpole' Phelps in *The Naval Treaty*) was enough of a *rara avis* to attract a certain amount of ironic ragging.

Do you wonder at my temerity in allowing such definite statements to drop from my hero's lips—as the steamer furrows its quiet way across the dark blue circle of the sea? Have no fear, if my reviewers dispute them they will receive a crushing reply.

From Watson himself we learn in *A Study in Scarlet* that his father was dead and that he had no relations in England; observe he did not say that he had none elsewhere. That the family had emigrated to Australia and that it was from Australia the funds just sufficient for his own education arrived, is an easy deduction from a remark that he makes himself in telling the story of *The Sign of Four*. You remember in that story that the sight of the dug-up grounds of Pondicherry Lodge instantly reminds him of the excavations on the side of a hill in Ballarat. Now he could not have visited Australia between his return to England from India and the date of that adventure, for during all those years he was living in Baker Street with Sherlock Holmes. It was therefore a recollection of childhood—of the years which preceded his school days with 'Tadpole' Phelps—which prompted the comparison. I just give this example to show that though my methods as a biographer may be modern, my conscience is that of the old-fashioned historian.

I will not trouble you with his rush to Afghanistan, nor with the battle of Maiwand and the subsequent relief of Kandahar by Lord Roberts' gallant march, though such incidents supply some of my brightest pages. It was at that disastrous engagement, to use Dr Watson's own words, that he was 'struck on the shoulder by a Jezail bullet which shattered the bone and grazed the sub-clavian artery'. He was 'removed to the base hospital at Peshawar', where he was healed of his wound, but caught enteric fever. I say healed, although—and this is an unexpected fact which a biographer must blindly accept—he limped for years afterwards, and in damp weather, as you well remember, was always apt to feel pain in his leg. He was invalided home on the troopship *Orontes* and he landed at Portsmouth towards the end of December 1880.

There was a dash of wild blood in the Watsons. We know from his elder brother's watch that he died prematurely from drink and in poverty, in spite of excellent abilities which enabled him intermittently to retrieve his position in the world. The first month or so of Watson's life after his return to England was a period to which he looked back with misgivings. The modern tendency in biography to emphasise the regrettable side of human nature may tempt to read more than is justifiable into that violent phrase which Watson employs in describing London—he speaks of it as 'that great cesspool into which all the loungers and idlers of the Empire are irresistibly drained'— but there can be little doubt that during the first two months of 1880, for the last time in his life, Watson sowed a few wild oats. The gods, Shakespeare says in his old-fashioned way, make scourges of our pleasant vices. It is more in harmony with the tone of modern biography to point out here that had not young Stamford of Bart's clapped Watson on the shoulder as he leant across the Criterion zinc talking to the barmaid, the latter would never have met Holmes.

As everyone knows, it was economy that first compelled the two friends to keep house together. Watson, with what may be called his superb normality, had found it impossible to line independently on his military pension of £209 6s. Economy was equally necessary in the case of the young Sherlock Holmes. We know that Mrs Hudson's charges were extremely moderate, but it seems scarcely possible that with food, light and fuel they could, even in the eighties, have been less than £5 a week. We know that Holmes's clientele was at first by no means wealthy, and that his artist's devotion to his profession often induced him to undertake cases which left him out of pocket. However, fame came rapidly, while Watson succeeded in placing his literary work. By 1888 all financial troubles were over.

There is in the records of his life what Henry James would have called a great straddling unaccommodating fact: he appears to have been married in two different years. This has led to the wildest surmises, even to the reckless suggestion that he kept two establishments. Apart from the importance of finding a solution from the point of view of clearing the character of Dr Watson himself, it is necessary to determine the precise year of his marriage if we are to arrange the stories in chronological order, since Dr Watson constantly used his own

marriage as a sort of B.C. or A.D. in recounting events. It is
The Sign of Four, of course, which gives us the circumstances
which led up to it. What was the date of this adventure? Before
discussing this point, which I warn you will require the application of all your arithmetical faculties, let me state what the
point at issue is: did Dr Watson marry Miss Morston in the
autumn of 1887 or of 1888? There is evidence for both alternatives. I brush aside as frivolous the suggestion that Watson
had two wives. The perfect character of Mrs Watson, who not
only never kept him from his old friend, but even encouraged
him to jeopardise his practice by continually going off upon
'adventures', are alone sufficient to refute it. Those who make
it may be acute reasoners but they know little of matrimony
and nothing of bigamy—its cause and cure.

Let us bend our minds for a moment to this question of dates
and weigh the evidence. In *A Scandal in Bohemia* which is
expressly stated to have occurred in March 1888, Watson is
already married. He was about to be married in a few weeks
when the events described in *The Noble Bachelor* took place.
And the date of that story is fixed by Holmes' reference to
Lord St. Simon's age—'Born in 1846, he is forty-one years old'.
It is, therefore, the autumn of 1887. This is the case for fixing
Watson's marriage in the autumn of that year. Now let us
examine the case of those who favour the view that he was
married in the autumn of 1888. *The Sign of Four* gives us, as
every schoolboy knows, the circumstances which led up to his
marriage. When Miss Morston called at Baker Street with the
letter asking her to be at the third pillar from the left outside
the Lyceum that night, Holmes asked to see the envelope:
'Postmark, London, S.W. Date, July 7. Hum!' he remarked;
the date of her visit was therefore July 8. Nor is the year
apparently less certain. 'About six years ago—to be exact,
upon the 4th of May, 1882—an advertisement appeared in
The Times asking for the address of Miss Mary Morston', she
also told him. From her words 'six years ago' many have concluded that *A Sign of Four* must be assigned to 1888.

But those who think so have failed to notice one significant fact. From May 1882, onwards, every year, on the same day Miss Morston had received 'a very large and lustrous pearl' from an unknown benefactor. If, as she asserted, the first had arrived on 4th May, 'six years ago', she would have received by 7th July 1888, seven pearls. Mark that. But the box she showed Dr Watson only contained '*six* of the finest pearls he had ever seen'. Is it not the more reasonable to suppose that Miss Morston habitually used the words 'about so long ago' a little vaguely (she was clearly fond of using the phrase, for in a short conversation she uses it twice), than that she had lost a pearl and said nothing about her loss? It seems to me far safer to trust the evidence of the pearls themselves than her hasty estimate of the number of years which had passed since she began to receive them, and in that case the otherwise sinister implications deducible from *A Scandal in Bohemia* and *The Noble Bachelor* entirely disappear. There is another reason for not laying too much stress upon the complete verbal accuracy of all statements in *The Sign of Four*. Dr Watson during his short and passionate courtship was thrown into great confusion of mind. Holmes (you remember) declared afterwards that he had overheard him caution the unhappy Sholto against the great danger of taking more than two drops of castor oil while he recommended strychnine in large doses as a sedative. We need not therefore be *very* surprised that Dr Watson in recounting the events of that evening of 8th July should, in writing his account of it afterwards, say 'it was a September evening and a dense drizzly fog lay low upon the great city'. No. A story so evidently written in a hubble-bubble of emotion must not be used, and the reputation of one concerning whom every reader feels that whatever record leaps to light he ought never to be shamed, is saved.

BLOOMSBURY
AN UNFINISHED MEMOIR

1933

'BLOOMSBURY' is a regional adjective which has been used as a label for a few writers and painters who dwell, or have some time or other dwelt, in that part of London; and who used to, or do, see a good deal of each other. It is chiefly used as a term of abuse in reviews. In the shorthand of colloquial criticism and gossip it connotes, vaguely, a certain arrogant exclusiveness, anti-herd intellectualism, and a superior moral-frivolity. 'Bloomsbury', as a word, has also found its way into the jargon of French and German criticism of Contemporary English literature, where it takes on the significance of a literary movement. But in England, where spectators see, at any rate, that there is little in common between the work of Lytton Strachey, Virginia Woolf, Clive Bell, David Garnett, Roger Fry, Maynard Keynes, Leonard Woolf, Vanessa Bell, Duncan Grant, E. M. Forster, it does not suggest so much a movement as a 'push'; a mutual-admiration society, to which some, suffering from suspicion-mania, have attributed a sinister power over the Press. Writers and painters who are indignant, sometimes rightly, sometimes wrongly, at their works not meeting with universal praise, and looking about for an explanation of the inexplicable, have been known to mutter darkly 'Bloomsbury' and find relief.

> Of all the clever people round me here
> I most delight in Me—
> Mine is the only voice I hear,
> And mine the only face I see.

Roy Campbell's epigram, which he calls *Home Thoughts in Bloomsbury*, expresses a conception of it which is only an exaggeration of one that is fairly common. But, in fact, 'Bloomsbury' is neither a movement, nor a push, but only a group of old friends; whose affection and respect for each other has stood the test of nearly thirty years and whose intellectual candour makes their company agreeable to each other. It never was a movement. In taste and judgment 'Bloomsbury' from the start has been at variance with itself. Indeed, here lay its charm as a social circle. There was enough mutual respect and affection, well tested by time, to supply cement; enough difference of temperament and opinion to stimulate talk; enough intellectual honesty to enable them to learn from each other. Their association began when they were far too young (with the exception of Roger Fry) to have achieved anything; and by the time the world heard of 'Bloomsbury', 'Bloomsbury' as a group had ceased to exist. Though old ties remained, friends were scattered; and most of them were seeing much more of new friends than of each other: 'Marriage and death and division make barren our lives.'

And so far from being a mutual admiration society, 'Bloomsbury' is the last place where a Bloomsburian, who has just written a book, would look for that enthusiastic amazement at his achievement which authors enjoy most. A considerate silence, a carefully measured commendation veering at once into a discussion of generalities, is the most he, or she, ever hopes to get *there*. In early days, before they had done anything, they did believe in one another—perhaps more than each believed in himself or herself.

'Bloomsbury' has never been a spiritual home to me; but let me add that I have not got one, although at Cambridge for a few years I fancied that I had. 'Bloomsbury' had been to me, rather, what those who cater for sailors (like theirs, my home is a floating one) call 'a home from home'. Looking back I see that I converged upon 'Bloomsbury' by three ways: through making friends with Clive Bell, through getting to know some Cambridge 'Apostles' junior to me, and through my introduction into the home-life of Miss Vanessa and Miss Virginia Stephen. Although the second of these approaches was prior in time I will begin with my first encounter (it was strikingly accidental) with Clive Bell.

My undergraduate days were over, and I was going down to Cambridge one November afternoon in 1901 to visit George Moore, the philosopher, who still had rooms in Neville's Court. It must have been that train which gets us up to Cambridge in time for dinner. My mood was one of dejection; and when such moods come upon me I take any modest steps handy to relieve them. If I happen, for instance, to be travelling, and to have money in my pocket, I will travel first-class. It does me hardly any perceptible good, but still perhaps—a little. There was on this occasion one other occupant of the carriage that I entered that afternoon. He was a youth with a noticeable head of wavy auburn hair, and that milk-white skin which often goes with it. I cannot visualise him completely, but I think I am safe in saying that he was dressed with careless opulence, and that he wore, flung open, a dark fur coat with a deep astrakhan collar. I thought his appearance distinctly enviable, and I was prepared by my melancholy to take a pathetically unselfish interest in the good fortune of others. It was not his aspect which struck me as proclaiming him to be one of the fortunate; not even his youth, a quality, which, at the age of twenty-four, I thought even more enviable than I think it now, but his eager and enjoying temperament, with which in the first ten minutes of conversation I came in contact. I forgot in talk with him the weight of troubles, cosmic and private, which were oppressing me; and I fancied myself to be enjoying, vicariously at any rate, through him, the prospect of helping myself in a generous manner to the pleasures of life. My attitude towards this young man (it was inevitable in one so rent and bruised by experience as myself) was distinctly avuncular. Happily either he did not perceive this or he did not resent it. I delighted in him because I could see in imagination the enormous rich hunk he was about to cut from the cake of life. What we talked about I cannot remember, but that was the residual impression. I must, of course, have asked him if he did not know 'So-and-So, and So-and-So', mentioning those younger Cambridge 'Apostles' who, as I said, also proved to be roads leading to 'Bloomsbury'—Lytton Strachey certainly was one of them. Anyhow we got on so well together that he asked me to lunch with him the next day. One other thing interested me in him, the orientation of his life at the moment seemed to resemble what my own had been when I first went up to Cambridge.

He appeared to have a foot in two communities which, in the University, and indeed in the world itself, are separated from each other by as deep a trench as divides, say, Roman Catholics from the rest of mankind. He seemed to live, half with the rich sporting-set, and half with the intellectuals; and sure enough next day I found my host in a white hunting-stock and a dressing gown. His aspect was reminiscent of a sporting young man in a Leach picture at that delicious moment when he has pulled off his top-boots and is about to take his hot shower-bath. That it was a Sunday and he could not have thrown a leg over a horse that morning, added to his character a touch of fantasy, which was in harmony with my first impression of him.

ROGER FRY

1945

I

THE most analytical mind that has been applied to the study of the visual arts—I am thinking of Roger Fry as a critic. But meanwhile, I have been fluttering like a bird in a glasshouse, trying to get out into a past which I can see but cannot reach. Seeing is not enough: I can record facts, but I have little hope of transmitting his personality, or the quality of the many varied hours I spent in his company.

Though these were scattered over more than thirty years, they have left behind so unified an impression of him that I cannot believe I did not always know him well. His judgments sometimes took me by surprise, but never Roger Fry himself. Whatever he did or said, he remained the man whom I had already divined, and it was good to be near him.

The intimacy of our communication varied, as in a prolonged relation it always does, with the exigencies of life, which now draws friends close together—sometimes, indeed, bangs them together and not without bruises—now separates their intensest interests. But whether intercourse with him was on the level of discussion, or on personal matters, all who knew him will bear me out: you met with the same integrity of mind, the same Roger Fry, who could ultimately forgive anything except failure in candour, at moments when candour is necessary to arriving at a true judgment or disentangling a mutual predicament: a quality so valuable in personal relations and so necessary to the intellectual life. It was the intellectual life that he lived, the life of an artist in whom the intellect predominates.

If to remain 'young' is to keep a vivid curiosity, the power of enjoying the present, and a faith in pleasure (characteristics often lacking in youth), then it must be also said of him, to use an obituary *cliché*, that he remained 'young to the last'. And if to grow 'old' is to become fussy and cautious and cosy, then, certainly, he had a horror of old-age. He was a most energetic man, and he contested every curtailment of activity which years inevitably bring. I sometimes thought he was spending his energies too freely, and I used to protest: 'Roger, it's no use clinging to every bannister when Father Time is determined to kick us downstairs.' But he was probably right; it is not much use hoarding life. I worked with him, travelled with him, played with him; and though to say this may suggest something I do not intend, looking back, I do not remember any great difference between either working, or travelling, or talking with him. It was the strenuous pleasure he took in things that stands out in retrospect. The strenuousness of his delight in works of art is clearly seen in his criticism; it animated also his enjoyment of food, talk, travel, and the way he set about practical projects. It was gloriously exhilarating. Though it might be sometimes fatiguing to weaker spirits, thanks to a little slyness and to his own sense of fun, I, for one, never had any difficulty in relaxing the pitch of concentration when this was necessary to my contentment, or in mitigating the impetuosity of his plans.

He was a hedonist, but a hedonist of a peculiar kind. For those who never saw him, the most rapid way of suggesting his appearance is to say that it was easy to imagine him dressed as a fasting friar in a brown habit with a rope round his waist. He would have looked the part perfectly. There was not a touch of grossness, either of the over-fastidious or the over-greedy kind, in his love of pleasure. It was a grateful love, and he believed in the wisdom of being happy. His voice—and his voice was one of the physical qualities which made him attractive—resembled Voltaire's; he had *une voix sombre et majestueuse*. He laughed very easily. In fact, he was more immediately moved by a sense of the absurdity of men and their opinions than by indignation at them, though after a moment or two's reflection indignation usually followed. He was an implacable anti-Philistine (I used to think sometimes he was too hard on the Philistines, who, after all, supply most of the vertebrae in the backbone of life); and like most anti-Philistines, he was a strong pacifist and a detester of fervid patriotism.

He had a great love of France, and since the failings of his own countrymen were under his nose, and he was rather reluctant to observe those of the French, he gave the latter the benefit in most comparisons. He valued highly their 'quick apprehension of life' (readers of *Characteristics of French Art* will recall the ingenuity and conviction with which he worked out in the history of their art the effects of this characteristic); he loved their conscious and discriminating hedonism and their ubiquitous sensitiveness to the *mise en valeur*. He could speak their language well, and even lecture effectively in French. He knew he had learnt more from modern French art than from the modern art of any other country, and it is a commonplace to say that it is chiefly due to him that English artists and amateurs now appreciate that art. And this brings me to the turning-point in his career—his organising of the famous Post-Impressionist Exhibition of 1910.

In a minor and entirely ancillary way I too was connected with it.

II

WHEN Roger Fry proposed that I should go abroad and help assemble a representative exhibition of pictures by Cézanne, Matisse, Van Gogh, Gauguin, Seurat, Picasso and other now familiar French painters (incidentally he promised me a few days' bicycling in France) I don't think he chose me because he had special trust in my judgment. Of course he knew I was fond of pictures and that if confronted with one I could look at it with interest for more than two minutes—a faculty not so common as you might suppose. (Next time you are in a gallery you can verify this by timing people as they go round.) And

then, though I could not generalise about artists, I did occasionally say something about a picture which would interest
him, though it might be only 'I'm almost sure that cow is too
near the tree'; or 'that crimson blob next her nose—of course,
I see something of the kind is necessary and I didn't notice it
at all at first, but now I have—it bothers me.' But what really
influenced him in choosing me was that we were happy together. My failings were not the sort which annoyed him, nor
(equally important) were my virtues. Masterful men often
prefer a rather incompetent colleague to an over-confident one.
Fry was capable of making muddles himself; he would not
have been quite comfortable with anyone implacably efficient.
And here I must mention that he was also a most persuasive
man.

Hearing that the Grafton Galleries had no show for the
months between their usual London Season exhibition and the
new year's, he proceeded to convince them that they might do
worse than hold a stop-gap exhibition of modern foreign artists
—also that Desmond MacCarthy was an excellent man of
business which indeed, in my opinion (but of this you must
judge for yourselves) he did turn out to be. It was all settled
in a tremendous hurry. I had just time to interview the director
of the Galleries. He apologised for the smallness of my fee (a
hundred pounds). But if—he added, with a pitying smile—if
there were profits, I might have half of them. Neither the
committee of the Grafton Galleries nor Roger Fry thought for
one moment that the show could be a financial success.

Then I was stricken down with an influenza. However,
Roger wasn't a man to be put out by a little thing like that.
He made me rise from bed, drink a bottle of champagne and
catch the boat for Calais with him. I arrived in Paris feeling
as though my head were about the size and weight of an apple.

Of course, the first people we went to see in Paris were
dealers who had modern pictures. If they could be persuaded
to lend, then the London show would be representative. We
spent day after day looking at the pictures, and nearly all those

which Roger preferred were at our disposal. I remember his raptures. He would sit in front of them with his hands on his knees groaning repeatedly 'Wonderful! wonderful!' I don't think at that date anybody in England possessed any specimens of these artists' works, except Sutro, the playwright, who had a small Van Gogh. At these interviews with dealers I used to pose as M. le Publique, and on one point my verdict was final: Was there, or was there not, anything in some nude which might create an outcry in London?

Then off we went for our little tour, after which Roger returned to London and I was sent on to Munich and Holland to get other pictures. In Amsterdam Van Gogh's sister, Madame Gosschalk Bonger, had, of course, many of her late brother's, and they were still admirably cheap. When we came to price them she was asking a hundred and twenty pounds or less for some admirable examples of his art. Then I returned to Paris to settle the business side.

Now, though I was supposed to be a man of affairs, when the biggest dealer asked me what percentage the Galleries wanted on sales, I confess I was floored. It was a point on which I had neglected to inform myself before starting. At a venture I murmured, 'twenty per cent', and he replied, '*Parfaitement, Monsieur.*' Then he went on, 'If you get an offer for a picture, do not communicate at once with the artist, but with me first. He may accept less and then we can share the difference.' Now the success of the exhibition largely depended on keeping on good terms with him. How would you have behaved? Well, I summoned up all the tact for which an aunt of mine had been famous, and replied: 'I don't think I can agree to anything not down in black and white, but if you write to me. . . . ' He looked a little hard at me and then repeated, '*Parfaitement, Monsieur.*' Of course, I never received that letter. We remained on excellent terms, and all was well.

On my return to London I reported that several hundred interesting pictures were available (transit insurance probably £150). I was told that expenses had to be kept down as the venture was a certain loss; still, one hundred pounds might be spent on advertising; *that* was satisfactory. I was about to leave when the director casually remarked: 'I suppose you secured our usual percentage on sales?' Feebly, I murmured: 'You never told me what it was.' There was an oppressive pause. 'Do you mean to say you didn't ask if you didn't know? What *did* you get?' 'Twenty per cent.' 'Twenty? Why, we've *never* got more than eleven!' For several days after that I was convinced that I was cut out for a business career.

What was the exhibition to be called? That was the next question. Roger and I and a young journalist who was to help us with publicity, met to consider this; and it was at that meeting that a word which is now safely embedded in the English language—'post-impressionism'—was invented. Roger first suggested various terms like 'expressionism', which aimed at distinguishing these artists from the impressionists; but the journalist wouldn't have that or any other of his alternatives. At last Roger, losing patience, said: 'Oh, let's just call them post-impressionists; at any rate, they came after the im-pressionists.' Later he handed over to me, with a few notes, the ticklish job of writing the preface to the catalogue—the unsigned preface. This work of mine was far more widely quoted than anything I was ever destined to write, and phrases from it like 'A good rocking-horse is more like a horse than the snapshot of a Derby winner' were quoted and re-quoted with laughter.

The hurried agonies of that picture-hanging are still vivid to me. Roger was entirely absorbed in deciding which picture would look best next another, while it lay with me to number them. As he was continually shifting them about when I was elsewhere, I was terrified that the numbers and titles wouldn't always correspond, with the effect of increasing the mockery, which I now felt certain the exhibition would excite. It was four a.m. before I got to bed the night before Press day, and then I couldn't sleep for worrying. When the newspaper was brought to me with coffee in bed, although it happened to

contain a long and laudatory review of a book I had just
published, I couldn't even read that. The prospect of public
ridicule owing to having, say, catalogued a nude girl as 'Station-
master at Arles', made my walk to the gallery more like a walk
to the gallows. Soon after ten, the Press began to arrive. Now
anything new in art is apt to provoke the same kind of indignation as immoral conduct, and vice is detected in perfectly
innocent pictures. Perhaps any mental shock is apt to remind
people of moral shocks they have received, and the sensations
being similar, they attribute this to the same cause. Anyhow,
as I walked about among the tittering newspaper critics busily
taking notes (they saw at once that the whole thing was splendid
copy) I kept overhearing such remarks as 'Pure pornography',
'Admirably indecent'. Not a word of truth, of course, in this.
As M. le Publique I had been careful to exclude too frankly
physiological nudes and, indeed, at the last moment, instead
of hanging two of the pictures, I told Roger they had better be
kept, for a time, in my sanctum downstairs.

The Press notices were certainly calculated to rouse curiosity.
And from the opening day the public flocked, and the big
rooms echoed with explosions of laughter and indignation.
Sometimes I hovered about trying to explain what I thought
was the point of a picture, drawing attention to colour or
arrangement, and here and there, now and then, I did find a
receptive listener. One young lady seemed to come nearly
every day for a lecture and presently proposed to me, which
was almost a fault in the opposite direction. I hit on a device
for calming those of the furious who stormed down in a rage
to my sanctum beneath the galleries. To these I would first
explain that I was, after all, only the secretary, so I could not
very well close the exhibition on my own initiative that very
evening. But I would add, 'Your point of view is most interesting, and if you will write it down and sign it, I shall be most
happy to pin it up in the entrance for all to read.' This suggestion acted as a sedative. The indignant one would reply, 'Oh,
I don't know that I want to put anything on paper; only I did

feel that what I have said ought to be said.' Occasionally I did get a document to pin up. I wish I had kept them.

The people who annoyed me most were, I think, cultivated women who went deliberately into trills of silvery laughter in front of pictures. With those who were genuinely amused I had some sympathy. I remember, for instance, a stout, elderly man of a good appearance, led in by a young woman, who went into such convulsions of laughter on catching sight of Cézanne's portrait of his wife in the first little room that his companion had to take him out and walk him up and down in the fresh air. When they re-entered, I watched him going round the other rooms, where there really were some startling pictures. He did so without a smile. Now when one has laughed oneself weak, one can't laugh again even at something far funnier. This man's amusement had been genuine, not wilful, or superior, or offensive, and I forgave it.

Presently we actually began to sell pictures. The Art Gallery at Helsinki bought a very fine Cézanne for £800, I remember; and when we closed, my share of the profits amounted to— what do you think?—over £460—such a lump sum as I had never earned before, and would never earn again! Not only had the exhibition been the theme of non-stop correspondence in the papers and of pamphlet wars—all the best known painters were, alas, against us—but it also provoked lectures from mental specialists. Fry himself did not make one penny out of the exhibition, nor did he out of the Omega workshops, which he started seven years later. Indeed, by introducing the works of Cézanne, Matisse, Seurat, Van Gogh, Gauguin and Picasso to the British public, he smashed for a long time his reputation as an art critic. Kind people called him mad, and reminded others that his wife was in an asylum. The majority declared him to be a subverter of morals and art, and a blatant self-advertiser.

I believe few people know the position which he occupied in the world when he took this enthusiastic and disinterested step. After taking a double first in Science at Cambridge and resolving to make painting, which had been his boyhood's hobby, his profession, he earned his living as a journalist-critic. The years which followed his leaving Cambridge were those during which he laid the foundations of his wide and accurate knowledge of the history of Art. His paper was *The Athenaeum,* and it is a tribute to the quality of the articles which he then wrote, and which are still buried in back files, that in 1906, although he had only published in book form a short monograph on Giovanni Bellini and a preface to Sir Joshua Reynolds's *Discourses* (1905), he should have been appointed in the following year to the Metropolitan Art Gallery in New York. And it is worth mentioning that immediately after he had accepted the American offer he found he might have had the Directorship of the National Gallery.

He was thus already right at the top among European connoisseurs and art critics. His judgment carried weight in the world. What was it that enabled him to sacrifice such a position without a backward glance of caution? It was not courage, but something rarer—an instinctive and instant response, a joy in discovering the unrecognised beauty. This power of making discoveries was connected with a noticeable trait in him, which was even amusingly at variance with his strong intellect. He was a credulous man. There were moments when I used to exclaim, 'You would be the greatest of critics if you only sometimes listened to the small still voice which whispers "Fiddlesticks!" '

And it was not only in matters connected with Art that this showed itself. He would entertain, at any rate for a long time on approval, notions connected with quackery of all sorts— intellectual, medical and psychical. In that respect he resembled William James, who was capable of giving any crank in philosophy, though he might lack the most obvious credentials, enthusiastic attention. Roger Fry also was always ready to believe that someone had done something or was following something which might prove immensely important. Darwin used to indulge in what he called his 'fool experiments', as when for example he would play a trumpet to his plants. The entirely sensible never discover anything. There is no doubt that to this openness of mind and imagination Roger Fry, in an entirely different sphere, owed his discovery not only of mare's nests but of things of the utmost importance to Art and artists.

It has been said since his death that as a painter he would have achieved better things had he not, while painting, known so well what he was doing. I do not think myself that that is the right analysis. In so far as he failed as a painter (and I feel confident that his work will be rated far higher than it is at present) it was due rather to that strenuousness of nature which I have already mentioned. It was difficult for him to remain passive before an object long enough. He was an extremely rapid worker, and his alertness enabled him to see *possible* pictures in every direction, not always in fruitful ones.

If, as I hope, specimens of his lifework as a painter are exhibited,* it will be seen that every phase of his sensibility as a critic found reflection at different times in his own performance. As a painter he tested himself what had excited him as a critic. To mention in conclusion one more personal characteristic, one which perhaps will hold together the sketch I have endeavoured to draw: he bore with magnanimity the indifference to his own work of younger artists whom he had praised and taught. That is very difficult to do without a little resentment —only possible to a profoundly disinterested man.

* An exhibition of Roger Fry's work was held in 1952 and Sir Desmond MacCarthy wrote the introduction to the catalogue.

PET MARJORY

1945

CHILDREN are a subject on which I can speak with some authority as I have been a child myself. Later on, I had three children of my own—nice ones—and when a parent I discovered what was the most charming thing about children —they're so easy to make happy, so quickly pleased. Thus in their company the adult enjoys, on exceptionally easy terms, the sensation of being himself or herself the best of company. With children, one's small jokes, perhaps hardly good enough for general circulation, have an instant and tremendous success. What's more, they can be repeated with equal success. And— joy!—so can one's stories! No need to watch a child's eyes for that glassy look. You can maunder on about what you did and saw either yesterday or twenty years ago, it will be received with the same flattering attention. And then how pleasant it is to be treated as a mine of undisputed, if inaccurate, information.

In a garden at evening you can exclaim: 'Look, look at the moon', without inspiring a nervous dread in your companion that you are about to turn poetical.

Yes, the enormous advantage of children's society is that we can be natural in their company.

Again, what a business it is giving a present to a contemporary. Would my friend like this or prefer that? And even if he would prefer that, isn't it the sort of thing he would rather choose for himself? Oh those questions! But almost any object will delight a child—a box, a bright clean tin, a bottle of red ink, a nice tight white roll or cord—I've had a success with old brass door nobs—and of course anything that bangs, squeaks or toots will do. And compare in the two cases the reception: with your friend, the moment of transfer is often one to be got through as quickly as possible. And it's almost shamefaced if the object happens to be expensive. 'I'm sure', says he, 'It's most awfully good of you. . . . ' 'Oh I only thought. . . . ' 'But you really oughtn't to have—hrrm, hrrm. Indeed I'm . . . ' 'Yes, yes,' the donor nervously interrupts, 'only I knew you'd . . . ' and then hastily 'Oh! aren't you going away next week?' Ouff! the relief! The transaction's over, and you're both back on the familiar footing. If the recipient is a woman, perhaps she'll say, 'It really *is* sweet of you. Now I *must* give you your tea'—and that's that!

Now recall what it's like giving a present to a child! One of two things happens, either whoop! a radiant creature is in your arms, or it stands solemnly taking stock of the object and, later, while you're thinking of other things, lo! a small silent figure stands at your elbow still holding the object, suggesting perhaps a shade of reproach, as much as to say, 'You've forgotten the little box.'

Oh, there's no doubt to whom, children or grown-ups, it is most *rewarding* to give a present. I don't wonder that children are popular, though of course we know (especially since the psychologists have been analysing them) that like ourselves they are festering with wickedness. But that doesn't matter a bean. They're lovable and make us happy, so much so that if you see a small white arm lying on the road after a blitz, a rage, not merely against your country's enemies, but the idiocy of mankind, boils and bubbles in your breast.

There is only one child in the English *Dictionary of National Biography*, Marjory Fleming, who died in her ninth year in 1811.

About fifty years later a journalist called Farnie (like her, a native of Kirkcaldy, in Scotland) published extracts from her journal. He called his pamphlet 'Pet Marjory: the story of a child fifty years ago'. I've never read it, but I am prepared to trust her more recent editor, Mr Esdaile, that everything readable in it is Marjory's own. 'She seems', he says, 'to have been visited by a premonition of her first biographer when she observed in her journal that "a great many authors have expressed themselves too sentimentally".'

It was Farnie who invented the name 'Pet Marjory', for she was known to her family as Madie, Madgie, or Muffy. But it was Dr John Brown, the author of *Rab and his Friends*, who made her famous. John Brown has been reprinted in *Everyman's Library*. He made Marjory live again, quoting her freely and now and then altering her text. The late Mr Frank Sidgwick, another of Marjorie's editors, has told us that in her famous poems on 'The Turkeys' and on 'The Charming Pug', Brown sometimes improved her rough lines. Marjory's most famous couplet is about the turkey who lost her three chicks:

> But she was more than usual calm;
> She did not give a single dam.

But these trifles are only grave in the eyes of scholars whose appreciation takes the form of treating a child's text with excessive reverence. After all, it is really thanks to Dr Brown alone that we are acquainted with this brilliant child.

He was an artist in his sentimental way, and he saw what a delightful subject she would make if only there were another sympathetic figure in the picture. Walter Scott knew her, and nothing suited his canvas better than to portray Marjory as Scott's 'pet'. Scott was related to the Keiths, who were related to Marjory's mother. But both Esdaile and Sidgwick, Marjory's recent editors, have thrown doubt on the pretty embroideries which John Brown wove round the child and the novelist. His readers will remember how his account of Marjory Fleming begins.

We are watching Walter Scott, who has just taken up *Waverley* again, walking from the Parliament House in Edinburgh back to his home, and then sitting down in his large green morocco elbow-chair, in front of his writing apparatus. Next Brown imagines him discovering that he is in no mood for writing, and exclaiming: 'I can make nothing of *Waverley* today; I'll awa' to Marjory.' So Scott makes his way through

a snowfall to the house of his friend Mrs Keith, with his dog
Maida at his heels. He takes the child home, wrapped in his
plaid, and the two remain together for 'three or more hours,
making the house ring with their laughter'. First, Scott has
to say his lessons, repeating nursery rhymes till Marjory
is satisfied that he is word-perfect; then 'he would read
ballads to her in his own glorious way, the two getting wild
with excitement over "Gill Morrice" or the "Baron of Smail-
holm"; and he would take her on his knee and make her repeat
Constance's speeches in *King John* till he swayed too and fro,
sobbing his fill'. Dr Brown asks us to imagine 'the little
creature drawing herself up to the height of her great argument':

> I will instruct my sorrows to be proud
> For grief is proud, and makes his owner stout,
> Here I and sorrow sit.

'Scott used to say', Brown adds, 'that he was amazed at her
power over him, saying to Mrs Keith, "She's the most extraordinary creature I ever met with, and her repeating of Shakespeare overpowers me as nothing else does." '

Of course there is writing-up in all this; it's the product of
imaginative expansion. And yet for my part I shall continue to
see this engaging child where I first found her—on Walter
Scott's knee—although Marjory only mentions Scott once, and
then only as the author of her favourite ballad 'Helvellyn',
while he never mentions her at all in any of his letters.

Now here is a letter from Marjory herself to her elder sister.

My dear Isa, I now sit down on my bottom to answer all your
kind and beloved letters which you was so good as to write to me.
This is the first time I ever wrote a letter in my life. There are a
great many Girls in the Square and they cry just like a pig when we
are under the painful necessity of putting it to Death. Miss Potune
a Lady of my acquaintance praises me dreadfully. I repeat something
out of Dean Swift and she said I was fit for the stage and you may
think I was primed up with majestic Pride, but upon my word I
felt myself turn a little birsay. Birsay is a word which is a word that
William composed, which is— as you may suppose—a little enraged.

This horrid fat simpleton says that my Aunt is beautiful which is entirely impossible for that is not her nature.

And now listen to her poem on her monkey:

> O lovely O most charming pug
> Thy graceful air and heavenly mug.
> The beauties of his mind do shine
> And every bit is shaped so fine.
> Your very tail is most divine,
> Your teeth are whiter than the snow.
> You are a great buck and a beau.
> Your eyes is of so fine a shape,
> More like a Christian's than an ape.
> His cheeks is like the roses bloom.
> Your hair is like the raven's plume.
> His nose's cast is of the Roman,
> He is a very pretty woman.
> I could not get a rhyme for Roman
> And was obliged to call him woman.

Both her latest editors quote a passage from one of Stevenson's letters, 'Marjory Fleming was possibly—no, I take back possibly—she was one of the noblest works of God'. That is an outburst excusable in a letter, but to quote it solemnly seems to me a mistake. If it were possible to make me hate children some ecstatic child-worshippers would do it; if it were possible to make Marjory Fleming dull it could be done by treating her as 'a classic'.

Marjory was a child-genius, and a natural one. Alas, they can also be manufactured. I trust no self-indulgent parent listening will take the hint of how to do it from what I am about to say, for the process is not good for children; a child can be made, temporarily, into a genius in two ways: either by making it precociously self-conscious at an early age; or by retarding later its natural development. The first method works when the child has excellent faculties and a sensitive, sympathetic temperament. By playing on this it can be made to say or even write many pretty, quaint, unexpected things, which when quoted are likely to rouse wondering envy in other parents.

But even if the child is slow or stolid, much the same results can be obtained at a later stage by forcing it to continue living in a dream-world when it is naturally becoming interested in humdrum realities.

Marjory Fleming was not subject to such treatment. She lived at a time when it was still considered the duty of children to grow up as quickly as possible, and she was born with a little battery of quick wits. She had a temper which she often found occasion to deplore, though now it even helps to make her attractive to us. She was a darling, but don't let us make too much fuss over her.

MAX BEERBOHM

1946

'I SHAN'T offer you the slightest assistance', he wrote, on hearing that the late Bohun Lynch intended to write a book about him. 'I won't read a single word until your book is published. Even if modesty didn't prevent me, worldly wisdom would. I remember several books about men, who, not yet dead, had blandly aided and abetted the author, and I remember what awful asses those men seemed to me thereby to have made of themselves. I, who am a hundred miles away from being great, cannot afford such luxuries. My gifts are small. I've used them very well, and discreetly, never straining them; and the result is that I've made a charming little reputation. But that reputation is a frail plant. Don't over attend to it, Gardener Lynch! Don't drench and deluge it! The contents of a quite *small* watering-can will be quite enough. . . . Oh, keep it little —in proportion to its theme.'

Bohun Lynch's book, alas, was not a good one. After that letter he doubtless did his best to find faults, but unfortunately those he discovered were not there. But that letter, will enable you to guess that Sir Max Beerbohm is a most sensible man.

When in August 1942 a young admirer of his, Mr Alan Dent, founded a 'Maximillian Society' to celebrate his seventieth birthday, I had the privilege of taking the chair. We entertained him with old music-hall songs and turns such as he loves. They were interpreted by those brilliant artists of 'Late Joys', who helped to keep up our spirits during the first two years of the war. We also presented him with a small cellar of vintage wines. It was one of the few occasions on which I have enjoyed making a speech. I remember saying:

We all, whatever the date of our birth, continue to be the children of that period when each of us came intellectually of age—I'm speaking of imaginatively receptive people. You, Max, and your oldest friends here, writers and painters, are children of the 'nineties. And one of the things for which your contemporaries are so grateful to you is that your skilled example as a writer has kept them aware that, in that respect, they were not unblessed. It was a period where it was easier than it became later to perceive that Art has some connection with beauty; that craftsmanship is as important in the arts as originality; and that in a writer humane detachment is possibly quite as valuable as a burning ethical or economic conviction.

You have been most loyal to our period; you have shown us that in literature, even a shallow stream should be forded as if it might at any moment prove to be deep; that in prose as well as in poetry even a hair can throw a shadow. As a servant of the Comic Muse, you, like Sterne, have also known how to invest with a little loveliness —a joke. Of the 'nineties you were 'the wise youth'. The years have taught you very little—

(At this point, I remember, a slightly startled look replaced on Max's countenance that becoming expression of mingled incredulity and gratitude which we all endeavour to wear while listening in public to our own praises.)

The years have taught you very little—you could not help being *then* almost as sensible as you are today.

(To my joy I thought I saw him give a little nod.)

Then, although every leader of taste admired your elegantly unspontaneous essays, there was already in them something disconcerting to the more luxuriously confident of nineteenth-century aesthetes. I wonder if a remark which Wilde made about you ever reached your ears: 'The gods', he said, 'bestowed on Max the gift of perpetual old age.' At the time, in your twenties, this jibe might possibly have made you a little uneasy—for a little while.

The explanation of it is that you could not be silly even about Art—or Oscar. Now the chief—perhaps the only—distinctive virtue of old age is an inclination towards tolerance; when that inclination is combined with the fastidiousness of youth—well, then we get a 'Max'.

I cannot say that I knew 'Max' as he has drawn himself at the age of nineteen. It must have been some eight years later that I first met him, though I already knew him by sight. I remember walking one night down Piccadilly behind that

G

high-hat with its deep mourning-band which he has recorded. It was then perched above a very long dark top-coat with an astrakhan collar. I like to think I followed their wearer with something of his own interest in 'types'. In a gloved hand this figure held an ebony stick with an ivory knob which, wonderful to say, has not yet been lost. I remember noting also the little black curl on the nape of his neck like a drake's tail. His walk was slow and tranquil, such as one could hardly imagine ever breaking into a run.

But it was at the house of Mabel Beardsley, Aubrey Beardsley's sister, that I first met him . . . and oh! I was never going to let him go. He had replaced Shaw as dramatic critic on the *Saturday Review*, and he was living with his charming eager old mother and two of his sisters in a little house in Upper Brook Street. There I often visited him. Only on the very day when his copy was due was he invisible; for like myself, who had by then also become a dramatic critic, he needed the spur of dire compulsion to exchange the pleasures of thought for the pains of composition. He seemed to feel as I did that there was not very often anything much better to do with Time than to waste it rather fastidiously. His books are those of one who has always insisted on having leisure to observe. I put him right at the top of modern essayists.

The essays of Chesterton and Belloc are often like gusts of wind blowing off the hills of poetry, but my own kite will not always fly in that wind; it is liable to flutter, slant, and drop. In the hands of 'Max' I know it will be gently lifted and sail steadily for a while, pulling gently, with the scraps of criticism, ingenious comments on life and manners, tied to its tail, against a sky of calm contemplation. This is the function of the essayist. Or put it this way: he should find for us some inconspicuous turning which leads from the thoroughfare of every day into the garden of fancy or philosophy. He need not stop there; if he peeps in it is enough. Different he from the poets who with rhymes and rhythms, and extraordinary devices, peremptorily bid us put off our ordinary mood if we are to accompany them;

and against whom we feel in consequence no little resentment should they afterwards neither astound nor delight us. The transition from humour to serious reflection is always deftly managed by 'Max'; nor could anything in sentimental fiction be more finely touched than that scene in his story of 'William and Mary', where the story-teller pulls the bell of their empty house, tugs at it again and again, that he may hear repeatedly that quick sequence of notes, faint, far off, but so clear—and so like the dead woman's laughter.

It is the business of the artist in caricature to record what is comically characteristic and be true to his vision. He must have strong sympathies and antipathies and no respect for persons. 'Max's' own talent for caricature is the most intellectual in the history of English caricature. Compare it with the work of Gillray or of Rowlandson in the gross Flemish style of Jan Steen. The range of these old masters, however pretty in colour and animated in line, stretched little beyond the mere deformities of excessive fatness or emaciation; a guffaw at swollen thighs, exuberant bosoms, lantern-jaws, and round haggard eyes peering over a steaming dish—such was their stock-in-trade. The din, the racket, the monotony of such laughter! They set up to be satirists, but their own sense of the comic was itself that guzzling, roaring, man-and-woman-baiting kind of fun they satirised. Nevertheless they had the verve, skill, and thoroughness of artists; and when the horse-laugh dies out of English caricature, something vital and important dies with it. Caricature becomes half-hearted till it revives once more in Pellegrini and then in the implacable levity and literary subtlety of 'Max'.

Turn over one of his volumes of caricatures. How many are really literary or psychological *criticisms* presented in a visible dramatic form? They remind us that 'Max' is also one of the most accomplished of literary parodists. The parodies collected in 'A Christmas Garland' used to appear about Christmastime every year in the *Saturday Review*. I remember two of his victims confessing (they were Henry James and Arthur Benson), that after reading his devastating exaggerations of their respective mannerisms, they had been inhibited when they next sat down to write. 'Max' would have been almost more distressed than flattered to hear that his parody of Henry James had embarrassed for a week a writer whom he so much admired; but that he might have temporarily impeded the placid flow of commonplace from the gentle pen of Benson would have given him no pain.

To visit one of his exhibitions during his early period as a caricaturist was to gaze upon well-known figures at various stages of transformation towards the mechanical and grotesque; dandies dancing on their toes like puppets, or petrifying in starched shirts and resolutely buttoned coats; venerable statesmen appearing like creatures which loom for a moment through the green dusk of aquarium tanks; aesthetes drooping like tallow candles in too-hot air. As time went on, however, his methods changed, swerving in the direction of a comic portraiture, nearly wholly sympathetic in spirit, and away from pure caricature. Subjects in which his line was guided by aversion became rarer and rarer. His dislike of the hard vulgarity of Edwardian Society, typified often in the person of the monarch himself; his hostility towards noisy British Imperialism which was most intense during the Boer War, and was always visible in his caricatures (merciless) of Kipling, gradually changed to a more philosophic criticism of his age; a change which culminates in such a series of cartoons as those personifying the three centuries; wherein first the supercilious, clever eighteenth century is seen taking a pinch of snuff as he contemplates his stout, innocently-gaping successor, dressed in a chapel-going manufacturer's frock-coat; while he, in his turn, gazes in utter bewilderment upon his own offspring—a leather-clad, begoggled robot, racing with incredible speed into the unforeseen.

Yes, incredible as it might seem that anyone as mellow as young 'Max' should become mellower, as a caricaturist he certainly did.

In a caricature by Osbert Lancaster published in the *Strand*

Magazine for December 1946, 'Max' appears at a window. Osbert Lancaster has caught a characteristic attitude. He has duly exaggerated the lucid regard of those large grey heavy-lidded eyes. Here, decidedly is an old dandy, whom the young can regard as out-moded, though they had better beware of his mild scrutiny and the formidable civility of his wit. No doubt he 'dates'; of that he is proud. He looks easy to fluster, but he is really 'unusual calm'. Can you divine beneath the old pink and white face at the window, the dark round countenance of a rather melancholy Pierrot? It once was his. You will, I think, have no difficulty in attributing to the old gentleman a soft deliberate utterance, an almost soundless chuckle, and a manner quiet, though a shade more gesticulatory than is common. (Remember his half-brother was that imaginatively exuberant actor, Sir Herbert Tree.) But you cannot guess that all his life he has also been fond of a hoax, and ingenious in devising them. I am hoping that he will soon add to his delightful but too infrequent 'Talks', one on the art of hoaxing. I will not describe a little trap he once laid for me and into which, to his joy, I tumbled headlong.

But to suggest his impromptu gifts in that direction, let me recall one winter morning, when I was staying with him in lodgings at the seaside, and how he overcame my reluctance to rise. My bed was in a corner of the room, and you must imagine 'Max' standing at the window in his long white dressing gown, while I enjoy snuggling down under the blankets as we talk. Suddenly a remark of mine meets with no response; I notice on his face a look of grave delight. I repeat it, but he is silent. Then slowly, and in that literal tone with which we speak when really moved, I hear him say: 'That light! That grey and silver on the sea!' In an instant I am beside him and find myself face to face with a brick wall: *he had got me out of bed.*

His conversation, like his prose, is full of slight surprises. As a talker he belongs to more leisurely days, when the tempo of conversation permitted people to express themselves, and hosts did not prefer emphatic jawing guests, who shift their topic every moment. The art of conversation has passed away. In London to tell a story well is now impossible, for it may take more than two minutes; Oscar Wilde would be voted a bore, and neighbours at dinner would begin talking to each other after his third sentence.

'Max', it will not surprise you to hear, is, too, within a limited range, an excellent mimic, and not only of real people: he is also an impersonator. I have sometimes found I was no longer in *his* company, but in that of a dramatic critic whose accent was unrefined and whose mind was coarse, but who invariably contrived (confound him!) to hit nails on the head. I regret to say 'Max' always enjoyed my exasperation. ... But I have told you enough about the old gentleman who stares so gravely from his window.

IN PRAISE OF SPIDERS

1948

MOST of us are apt to neglect one easily available source of pleasure, which children wisely do not, namely the Insect World. I never watch a wasp devouring with throbbing eagerness my morning marmalade without feeling a touch of Jules Renard's sympathetic anxiety: 'Of course, she'll end by ruining her waist.' I enjoy, too, noting the inefficiency of industrious ants which has won them such a reputation, and to which Mark Twain alone has done justice. He took the trouble to watch the individual ant at work. It is one of my favourite passages in *The Tramp Abroad*.

Now I am devoted to spiders; their webs and their movements delight me. Why should I buy 'abstract pictures' when I can have for nothing in my window-pane such delicate designs, now drawn in threads of silver light, now in thinnest pencil? I love to see a spider swinging at the end of its line, in search of possible attachments for a web, and even more to watch it climbing up the empty air—a spectacle seemingly more miraculous than walking upon water.

We have, too, an enemy in common, the indomitable, unscarable house-fly, who, by the way, pest though he be to bald heads, is also mildly amusing to observe. I like to watch him sometimes rubbing his arms together 'in a queer sort of meditative mirth' or bobbing his head between them, to polish apparently his huge many-faceted eyes. But how right, alas, the Romans were to speak of 'having the courage of a fly'; the lion, indeed, is a coward compared with him. Think how the fly will return again and again and again to the charge, in spite of frightful risks, just for the sake of one sip of sweat or perhaps merely a little run on an agreeably smooth surface; contests in which man is almost invariably worsted; but not so spiders.

In return, I do my best to fight their battles against Feminine Power in the home. Why do women hate spiders so much, with whom after all they have a good deal in common? I suppose primarily because they associate neglect and dirt with them, and so conclude that their presence is derogatory. It is uphill work protecting spiders, and I have never been able to save one when it has made its web in a spare bedroom. Yet for a month or so I have sometimes succeeded.

The summer before last, for quite a while, I kept thirteen in my library and two (small ones) over my bed. The hopeful activity of those little creatures when I turned on my reading-lamp in the early hours of the morning was fascinating and pathetic. They fussed about, tugging at the ropes, thinking, I suppose, that it must be midday, and that there was at least the chance of a midge. But during my brief absence the window-cleaner's damp rag and that terrible feminine weapon the bunch of feathers at the end of a long cane did their fatal work: I was again spiderless.

Too few poets have done justice to the spider. There is of course the couplet by Pope which shows him to have a true appreciation of spiders:

> The spider's touch how exquisitely fine!
> Feels at each thread, and lives along the line.

And there is a beautiful passage in Whitman about them, and one less known by Blake which you will find in 'The Second Night of the Four Zoars'; a passage which, after asking a string of questions impossible to answer, continues:

> The Spider sits in his labour'd web, eager watching for the Fly:
> Presently comes a famish'd Bird and takes away the Spider.
> His web is left all desolate that his little anxious heart
> So careful wove and spread it out with sighs and weariness.

Like far the greater part of the Prophetic Books it is not good poetry but the feeling in it is charming.

Miss Jane Porter (1776-1850), who once enjoyed a European

fame as a novelist approaching that, say, of Agatha Christie, but is now only remembered as the author of 'Twinkle, twinkle, little star'—and then chiefly thanks to *that* having been parodied by Lewis Carroll—wrote, among her *Rhymes for the Nursery* a story in verse about a Spider and his Wife. It was as sad as Blake's lines, but with that added touch of heartless mockery— that ambivalence, the modern psychological critic would solemnly call it—which children particularly enjoy. Too many years have slipped away since I read it, but I remember the outline of the story and some verses. Mr and Mrs Spider had found a convenient cranny; they had settled their children in life and he, certainly, wanted to retire.

> He thought that the little his wife would consume,
> T'would be easy for him to provide her,
> Forgetting he liv'd in a gentleman's room,
> Where came, ev'ry morning, a maid and broom,
> Those pitiless foes to a spider!

Well, they were forced to move, and shortly afterwards Mrs Spider sent him back to the broken web for a wing or leg of fly. Unfortunately the gentleman saw him.

> Then presently poking him down to the floor
> (Nor stopping at all to consider),
> In one horrid smash the whole bus'ness was o'er,
> The poor little spider was heard of no more,
> To the lasting distress of his widow!

I know no other poems about spiders, and if anyone can direct me to more I shall be grateful. I do not count 'Little Miss Muffet', to whom indeed I attribute the unnecessary death of millions of spiders.

> I, singularly moved
> To love the lovely that are not beloved,

have attempted to write one, but it was not good enough; nor, alas, was the sonnet on a lobster, which, following boldly Victor Hugo, I addressed as 'the cardinal of the ocean.'

TWO SHORT REMINISCENCES

HENRY JAMES AND RUPERT BROOKE

READERS of Sir Edward Marsh's reminiscences, *A Number of People*, will discover before they have read far that he and I must have known each other for over forty years. I can judge *A Number of People* as impartially, I believe, as if it had not been written by so old a friend. I enjoyed it very much indeed—so much that I spread the reading of it over three days of my return voyage from America. What embarrasses me, however, is trying to allow for any added interest it may have acquired in my eyes from its describing so many people I know or have known, and from its references to incidents I remember myself—the meeting, for instance between Henry James and Rupert Brooke at Cambridge.

The mere mention of that occasion, when, by the by, the author was not present, called up a memory-picture of a Sunday breakfast-party in Maynard Keynes's rooms at King's. Henry James was still sitting at the table as I entered, with a cold poached egg in front of him bleeding to death upon a too large, a too thick, helping of bacon, and surrounded by a respectful circle of silent, smoking, observant undergraduates. I saw again his bright, hazel-grey, prominent eyes signalling distress to me in the doorway—a latecomer but an old acquaintance—and the flustered eagerness of his greeting. 'Tell me,' he said, as soon as we were outside, 'tell me about these remarkable young men, from whom, for some years past, I have received a most flattering annual invitation. The beauty of this gorgeous summer, the remembered beauty of this august place, and, to be frank, also a small domestic upheaval not unconnected with plumbing, has at last induced me, as you perceive, to respond. I naturally expected to provide the fox, to *be* the fox, if I may compare myself to so agile and wary an animal, but I never foresaw that I should have also to furnish the hounds, the horses, the drags, the terrier, the dog-carts—in short, the whole paraphernalia of the meet. Tell me, who was the long, quiet youth with fair hair who sometimes smiled?' 'His name', I replied, 'is Rupert Brooke and he writes poetry.' 'Any good?' At that time he had only published a few sentimental verses in the *Westminster Gazette*. 'No', I said. 'Well, I must say, I am *relieved*, for with *that* appearance, if he had also talent it would be too unfair. I should like to see him again.' That was arranged. Later in the day the novelist was punted by the poet through the Backs, and I afterwards asked Rupert what Henry James had talked about. 'He gave me advice; he told me not to be afraid of being happy.' It was sound advice to give any sensitive young man of Rupert Brooke's age; and it was, so it chanced, particularly applicable at that time to him.

THE QUEENSBERRYS

From a letter

... By the way, you're wrong about Bosie Douglas being crazy or his father either. Ld Q was sane; he was only an extravagantly self-willed, hard, old-fashioned nobleman who never cared two straws how eccentric he appeared or how miserable he made his wife and children. I used to meet poor Lady Queensberry sometimes. She wrung my heart; she had been gently, sweetly pretty. She looked as though she had been struck and was still quivering from the blow. You could tell she had once had a delicious sense of humour light as the skipping of rabbits by moonlight; but then she could no longer smile—only *laugh*, a faint little ghost's laugh. She liked meeting me because I would talk to her about her beloved Bosie who was then still under a black cloud. I had not met him yet. The first time I did so was some years later when Wilfrid Blunt gave a house-party at Newbuildings purposely to rehabilitate him. Douglas had married, and he thought it was really time people ceased to cut him. (W. B. had been very fond of his mother who was his cousin, and he liked Bosie too. Oscar he thought rather a figure of fun. He described to me a dinner of the Crabbet Club, which used to meet for one week-end every summer at his other house, Crabbet Park, drink till Sunday morning and recite poems and make speeches about each other's careers and characters. Curzon in introducing Oscar, the new member, made a speech so tactless and brutal in its chaff that poor Oscar turned crimson and could only stutter a few words in reply.)

But that is not what I wanted to remember. What I wanted to say was that Alfred Douglas was not in the least mad. He was one of the most charming people I have met—superficially —and charming in the way some boys are—even when he was well over forty. But, on provocation, he might become a festering mass of spite; and like all deeply vindictive natures he loved a fight. And true to his type, the out-law aristocrat, he was a very dirty fighter, not caring what weapons he used; and also caring precious little what means he took to get his way when in a tight place or wanting money. . . .

A MEMOIR OF YOUTH*

I N spite of having been at Eton and Cambridge I regard myself as a self-educated man, so little have I owed to those who tried to teach me. Yet it was at Cambridge that I acquired such faculties as I have possessed of making the most of life, and at Eton the worldly experience which may be a blessing or a snare. But neither at school nor at the university was the benefit to me. At school I was educated by the boys, at Cambridge by my friends—and myself.

I have not yet got very far in the story of my life. The last time I wrote I was on my way to Eton. Then I tried to describe the only time I have been in love after the manner of Dante, how at Paddington Station I saw a fellow new boy whom I instantly divined to be all I hoped I might become in the new world that lay before me. How I first postponed making his acquaintance till I should be more worthy of it—then abstained from doing so because that day seemed indefinitely postponed till, during my last term, passing him one Sunday afternoon in the Slough road, when I was something of a swell and he a nonentity, I turned back to ask him the time—thinking half cynically, half sentimentally, that it would be a pity to leave Eton without having once heard his voice.

But now let me go back, take up my tale from that moment when on Paddington platform the ideal was revealed to me in the person of a small brown boy, as quiet and gentle as a gazelle.

Both my parents were accompanying me down to Windsor for the entrance examination. In those days this was a mere form: no boy was ever ploughed. Even the Marquis of ——, who could hardly read and write and was entered that term at the bottom of the school, was not rejected, though, being found practically unteachable, he shortly disappeared. It was not my

*Written for the Memoir Club.

parents who occupied my thoughts on the journey, but that perfect boy who was to be my friend. My father and mother were to spend the night at The White Hart, Windsor, which stands opposite the round bastion of the curfew Tower of Windsor Castle, and from their bedroom window I gazed in ecstasy at it, for I adored castles. The gas lamps were already lit and the spring dusk deepening to darkness when we got into an old soft landau, drove down the steep curving street and over the river bridge where toll was taken, into Eton itself.

Although my name was down for Miss Evans' house, selected, and wisely as it proved, because the twelve Lytteltons had been there, I had to spend my first term at one of those small inferior houses which were kept by younger masters. It was one of the most ancient and decayed of the boarding houses, and accommodated only fifteen boys who at the time were under the control (so to speak) of a colourless, almost wordless, mathematical master who bore the spirited name of Allcock. The house stood on the site of the present School Library, and was faced with yellow plaster. It was only one storey high —with attics. In one of these my parents left me with my play-box, hamper and portmanteau. I was not, however, left long to unpack alone. The whole house was composed of new boys, with the exception of three upper-fifth-form boys who were to return on the morrow, and a boy who, having failed in Trials the term before, had been compelled to try again on the first day of this term. (More of him presently, but I may as well introduce him at once. He was called Cavendish and generally known as Ticky, a nickname dictated by a contempt which he thoroughly deserved.)

I was, as I said, not left to myself for long. I had barely begun to unpack and arrange my things when my attic was invaded by a number of little boys, who, although they were only my seniors by a few hours in the school, had the air of being perfectly at home, and whose high spirits were not in harmony with my own graver mood. No doubt my smile of welcome was a little sickly, but I opened my hamper under the usual questions—What's your name? How old are you? Going to be twelve soon. Golly, what a kid! What was your private school?—and handed round a tin of gingerbreads. But they and my *marrons glacés* were scorned on the first evening; the tummies of my visitors being already full of delicacies. They got better entertainment from some pictures I had brought to adorn my walls. My parents had spent that Easter in Rome and brought back photographs of some of the worst statuary in the Vatican. These, especially the fig-leaves on some of them, caused much amusement, in which I tried to join, though their interest in my wardrobe positively distressed me. Further pretence of seeing jokes I didn't see became impossible, and when one boy took up my nice hair-brushes with my monogram on them—a parting gift from my mother—and said, 'I wonder how these would look outside the window', an awful thing— or so I thought it at the time—happened. For a fragment of a second I must have lost consciousness, at least I was only aware of the sound of a smack, and something against my knuckles: I had hit him on the cheek. There was a roar of laughter. 'You little devil,' he exclaimed, with his hand to his face. But my contrition was so obviously genuine that instead of retaliating (in spite of cries urging him to do so) he allowed me to open the wash-stand and bathe his swelling eye.

I say I thought at the moment I had done an awful thing; that I had wrecked my chance of making friends for once and all, but it turned out a blessed mishap: I was never ragged again. Looking back, I see now that the boys who suffered most at a public school were either the proudly independent boys, or the half-cracked ones, like Jakes (about whom I may tell you something) or the hot-tempered who were good sport to tease, or the very gentle boys who would stand anything and became bullies' prey. A flash-in-the-pan temper, usually followed by remorse, was about the happiest endowment for getting through school on the pleasantest terms.

Then a bell rang and we all trooped down the stairs to supper in a pleasant low dining-room opening on a little garden, where

Allcock sat at the head of the table behind a round of cold roast beef.

Now Ticky Cavendish appeared on the scene. For a few hours he was in his glory. He was a large heavy boy in a tail coat, with a round white sweaty face, which, when not extremely dejected in expression, wore a zany half-smile. He was no good at games, not even at rowing—in spite of being a lout—and his company was inexpressibly dreary. But to-night, though we were soon to discover that he was of less consequence than any new boy, he was in virtue of size and seniority cock of the house. As we mounted the stairs again to go to bed, he stood at the top of them and slapped each of our faces as we passed with his podgy hand; a proceeding which we accepted as calmly as if it had been a recognised ceremonial salute. Two or three days later, if he put his moon face round one of our doors, the chances were that he would have been greeted with a shout of 'Get out, you slut!'

That night, after Allcock had stood for a moment rocking and hovering in my doorway and uttering at intervals 'Well, ah-rum, all right, good night, good night,' I knelt down in my little night-gown and recovered all my seriousness. It seemed almost frivolous to ask God for help in my exam next morning, after praying that I might become worthy to be the friend of the boy I had seen on Paddington platform, but I did— probably for my parents' sake.

The great mellow boom of the school clock striking the quarters and then the hours (sounds I was to come to love) seemed to be charged with the solemnity of the destiny before me, that of becoming almost perfectly good and in the end probably great.

It was a bright spring morning. The examination was held in upper school, where from each side the busts of Etonian statesman, each on its bracket above the dark panels carved with hundreds of names, looked down on a couple of hundred or so little boys scribbling desperately. The first paper was on the Scriptures. Except for my spelling, which consisted of improvised phonetics, I probably did rather well in that, for there was hardly a Biblical character from Doeg the Edonite and Tiglath the Pileezano to the Apostles I did not know something about. Then after breakfast there was another paper and then a break. My mother had returned to London, but my father, poor man, had stayed on to give me some good advice. And we walked up the High Street together (on the wrong side, I regret to say) to the station. He did not know exactly how to put what he wanted to say, so he left it very vague. But he did say, with an emphasis I thought rather odd, considering the comparative triviality of the matter, that I was on no account to go about with boys much older than myself. 'It is not', he added with some embarrassment, 'good form. So look out.' Well, I always took things from him, so that was that; but I wondered why he should make such a point of it. Like a sensible father, he had always confined himself to teaching me manners rather than words. I quite understood it was not good form. But he himself, dear man, as I was often to discover, sometimes to my cost, was ready to sacrifice 'good form' to many things—notably his own comfort. Only a year and month or so onwards from that very day, he was destined to appear at a Fourth of June—in a cap! My uncle and he had hired a launch, and nothing would have induced my father to submit to a frock-coat and top hat on the river, like other parents. Yet he would not miss the procession of boats either. So there he was, his white hair escaping from a deer-stalker, strolling about and joking among all the fashionable parents on the river bank, long before darkness could cover his and my shame. And he was the man whom I had once overheard advising another father about visiting his son at school: 'Mind, you must dress as carefully as if you were calling at Marlborough House.' The inconsistency of human nature was revealed to me very early.

So we kissed and I was left alone. I walked back, as I was to remember afterwards, with a shudder, again on the wrong side of the road. The entrance examination is very dim to me. I must have done well in arithmetic, algebra and Euclid, for on the knowledge of those subjects I had acquired before my twelfth year, I lived like a camel on its hump during my time at Eton, getting an alpha for them while a lower boy every term, and triumphantly passing the Little Go before coming up to Cambridge without adding a proposition of Euclid to my stock of them. I had been told by the Headmaster of my private school, the Rev. E. D. Stone, later himself an invariable winner of the Latin verse prizes in the *Westminster Gazette*, that the place I should take would entirely depend on my elegiacs. My Eton tutor was afterwards occasionally indulgent enough to describe my verses as 'interesting', but that was because they were a mixture of Virgilian phrases copied from a Thesaurus, plus a dog-Latin jocularity when I could not find any suitable tags. In the entrance examination my poetry must have been poor, for I only took middle fourth. (Imagine, however, my thrill on seeing 'Middleton', which was the name of my perfect friend, at the very top of the list; the only boy that year who had taken remove.)

What is, however, still vivid to me is a perplexingly impressive address from the Headmaster to us new boys in Upper School. Never had I seen so tremendous a man—or heard so heart-shaking a voice as that which proceeded from the vast chest of Dr Warre. There he stood, in the voluminous robe of divinity, its white tabs beneath his big jaw, his huge boots like the heads of baby hippopotami protruding from beneath its black silk skirts; a ruddy man, with short ginger hair, and pursed red lips which relaxed into a smile of formidable geniality as he gazed at us for a minute or so in silence—almost it seemed as if in affection.

Then the silence was broken by a baritone of unusual power and compass. He bade us welcome—it was awful; he hoped we would avoid all conduct that would bring discredit on the school—it seemed impossible. We must learn now or we should never learn that we were among the fortunate of the nation and that also implied responsibilities; some of us would perhaps be called to high positions, we must make ourselves worthy now. Above all—we must keep clear of the evil thing, that which defiles, and shun the abomination in our midst. His voice rose to a tenor cry. 'Have none of it, don't touch it, stamp it out.' And he went on to describe how he had been sometimes forced to send boys away on that account, and how one father had said to him that he would far rather he had been told his son was dead. This frightened me. My poor father, how agonised he would be if I should die, yet if I did something or other he would be still more miserable, and the horror of the situation was that I didn't even know for certain what it was. I might commit it by accident any day—like the sin against the Holy Ghost. But small boys are quick in putting two and two together, and I found myself sufficiently sure, in spite of the Headmaster's portentous vagueness, of what he was talking about, to feel relief at the end of his address. For, knowing what it was, I could avoid it and its awful consequences. And I may add that I did henceforth avoid it in spite of temptations, partly because it was wrong and largely because I was terrified of being sacked. As you may perhaps imagine, my interpretation was confirmed that evening when the other new boys at Allcock's talked over the Head's address with exuberant ribaldry which I could neither understand nor enjoy.

As time went on it became clear to me that this thing, this abomination in our midst, was next to games and, perhaps for a very few, their studies, the most important element in school life. When I say that, I am including its emotional off-shoots, which were of the most varied nature, grading up from prompt animalism through jokes to gay tenderness, even to restless passion and Platonic idealism. Some boys would be made happy for the day by a chance meeting, a few casual words exchanged. Others would discuss chances of seduction with the cynicism and aplomb of a Valmont. Distinctions in games, winning colours, might be coveted partly in view of the impression they could be counted upon to make upon 'the object'. I remember well the almost painful consciousness which possessed me when I walked out for the first time in my house colours. The atmosphere of the parade up town on summer evenings, when the boys in twos and threes (the swells arm in arm) slouched slowly past each other, with their hands in their pockets, their hats on the back of their heads, was precisely that of an esplanade. 'Good nights' and glances would be thrown about, and either shyly or eagerly returned.

Whatever the deficiencies of its curriculum, Eton certainly provided a sex education of remarkable range, and which, when segregation ceased, found (with nineteen out of twenty boys) its natural bearings. What is more, it included expressions from the feminine as well as masculine point of view. If I were a novelist, I should have no difficulty whatever in describing the mingled feelings of apprehension and exhilaration in a virtuous maid waiting upon a group of dazzling young swells: I should only have to recall my experiences as a fag.

But I am straying beyond my cadre—my first two days at Eton.

The first acquaintance I made (not counting the new boys at Allcock's) was Jakes. He was undoubtedly mad—not mad in the sense in which that word is applied by conventional people to anyone who is eccentric or independent, but insane in a strict pathological sense. It was a scandal that his parents should ever have dreamt of sending him to a public school. I don't think such criminal ignorance would be possible today. Why I picked him out among the ragging, chattering crowd of new boys who assembled in the school yard before each examination paper, I don't know.

I can't explain it, but all my life odd people seem to have either been drawn to me or I to them. And yet I consider myself to be particularly sane, and my esteem for common sense in others is, if anything, exaggerated. I put it right up among the tip-top virtues—on the whole I prefer it to genius. Yet there it is: certainly two of my most lasting and intimate friendships have been with men in whom that quality was conspicuously lacking. It was the same with my father. His only friend who survived from Cambridge days was a half-mad Hertfordshire squire, who was also a brilliant mathematician. When Arthur Giles Pullen arrived on a visit, declaring that he never felt better in his life, my parents used to look apprehensive. My mother's manner towards him was that of a lady leopard-tamer, confident yet watchful. His visits always contributed to the stock of family catch-words—for instance his roar of disgusted astonishment one morning at breakfast: 'What! No cold grouse on the sideboard?': or his calmer comment on a similar occasion: 'Yes, I always drink coffee as you all do, but I like to *see* tea.' However, I'm digressing.

Somehow or other then I found myself taking a walk with Jakes. His conversation was decidedly queer, but though I knew of course that there were mad grown-up people, I had then no idea that there were boy lunatics—until at the end of our stroll about south meadow, Jakes asked me up to his room. He said he had something secret to tell me. After closing the door, he seemed to forget what it was. Then he took out a pen knife, opened the blade and passed it rapidly three or four times through the key-hole. I asked him why he had done that. He said he thought someone might be peeping through it. I did not stay much longer with him, and I never learned his secret.

I used to see the poor little wretch at lower boy 'Absence' sometimes after that. He must have purchased more top-hats in a short term than any other Etonian, for it became a sort of ritual to bash in his before he could answer to his name, when he would sadly remark, 'That was my Fourth of June hat.'

His school career was luckily a short one. He disappeared in mid-term and I heard from a boy in his house what had led to it. The other boys discovered that Jakes was terrified of ghosts, and they told him that the best way of keeping them out of one's room at night was to cover the outside handle of one's door with marmalade. When his housemaster, going on his good-night rounds, first got a handful of the stuff, he thought it was an impertinent practical joke and Jakes was severely punished. But when he discovered that no punishment would induce Jakes to abandon the practice, it at last dawned on him that such a boy was proof against even the healthy normality of public school life, and Jakes was removed.

I think I said at the beginning that I owed to my public school a good deal of worldly knowledge. That was of course imbibed gradually, but even during those first three days I began to learn something in that direction. I have mentioned how Ticky Cavendish fell from his high estate the moment fifth form came back, and how so far from being able to smack our new-boy faces he hardly dared show his own in our rooms. I saw the same rapid re-shifting of status going on all round me during the next few weeks. Boys who had hectored and peacocked about with rollicking confidence turned into nonentities, and others rose in prestige. Thus from my twelfth year onwards I became gradually immune from being impressed by those, who, within restricted conditions, cut a dash; and useful this has proved: my snobbishness, such as it is, has been intelligently directed.

Ticky—to end up with the first boy I mentioned—Ticky I must also thank for having provided me with a peep into the process of sinking socially, in spite of being buoyed up by gigantic corks—a fortune in his case of over £200,000. This he ran through within two years of his coming of age.

And with this episode I will conclude.

After leaving Allcock's at the end of the half and going to Evans', I never spoke to Ticky again, until I was an uninvited guest at his flat in Piccadilly the summer after I had left Eton. (He was almost three years older than I was, as you may have gathered.) It came about this way, a way that was slightly shocking to me in that it revealed a mercenary side to some of my old Eton friends which hitherto was entirely unsuspected.

In Bond Street I ran up against Tubby Robertson, one of the most debonair and popular of Eton swells of my time. He asked me how I was spending the evening, and, hearing that I didn't know, said, 'O, come along, let's dine with Ticky Cavendish.' 'What!' I said, 'Ticky?' 'Oh,' he replied, 'Ticky is really not half a bad sort. Come along.' 'But,' I said, 'I haven't spoken to him for years. I can't . . . uninvited.' 'That doesn't matter. I've often taken a woman round there for the night, when I hadn't enough for a hotel bed. Other fellows you know are sure to be there.' And so they were, five or six of them who a year or two before would not have touched Ticky with a barge-pole. There they were, sure enough, drinking his champagne, bolting his delicacies and—so Tubby whispered of one or two of them—occasionally touching him for a pony or a monkey.

Ticky gave me his old sickly smile and seemed to think there was nothing odd in my sudden appearance. When I pass on a 'bus the Renaissance bay window of the room where we dined, from time to time, and for a moment or two, I recall that evening. We were waited on by two of the most villainous, greasy-eyed valets I had ever set eyes on, while Ticky at the head of the table was completely ignored by his guests, till the question arose what we should all do that night. Then turning to one of the valets he asked for some cash. The man put his hand in his trouser pocket and brought out a handful of gold, silver and crumpled notes, from which Ticky took what he thought would be necessary, and forth we went to see *The Belle of New York*.

Two things about Ticky should be told. Firstly that he was just back from a journey across Africa from Zanzibar to the West Coast, and secondly that in his mooney dank way he was much in love with Edna May, who was all the rage as The Belle.

The journey had proved, I afterwards heard, enormously, incredibly expensive, much more so than Edna May—alas! for Ticky—whom the largest fortune could hardly sugar.

He had fallen into the hands of a scoundrel of some experience as an explorer, who had demanded an open cheque every time the expedition crossed a river, on the threat of leaving Ticky stranded in darkest Africa. Ticky signed the cheques without too much misgiving, because he counted on stopping them on reaching civilisation again. But the explorer was up to that, and at the last river left Ticky on the opposite side of the bank, while he himself went on ahead and cashed them.

So here he was back again, thousands and thousands of pounds out of pocket, with a few sporting trophies and a pseudo-reputation as a traveller. His infatuation with Edna May had led to his permanently engaging a box and six stalls at the theatre. Thither we now proceeded. It is almost moving to recall the frantic clapping with which he himself greeted her appearance on the stage, and which he urged us also to supply.

Afterwards Tubby and I and Ticky went round to her rooms in the Holborn Hotel. Tubby was courting in his nonchalant way Edna's much plainer sister. Ticky had brought with him as symbols of his devotion four elephants' feet mounted in silver. They lay disregarded in a corner of her gaunt high sitting-room.

Her desire as she pecked at her supper seemed to be to get rid of him as soon as possible. Presently she did. After the door closed, his round face appeared again for a moment, and he addressed me in accents more melancholy than minatory, 'Keep off the grass.' They were the last words I ever heard from his lips.

Of course to me, a chaste youth of eighteen and an aspiring intellectual, the situation was highly, not to say embarrassingly exciting. She asked me to pour her out some champagne. If I were a modern poet, one of those who expect the world to thrill in response to a phrase which for them calls up a whole scene, I should conclude that there is immortal magic in the words, 'and the foam ran over her rings.'

She was very pretty indeed, but her beauty was of the plaintive kind, such as might grow upon one but hardly take one by storm.

Let me note as a change in manners—these were the days when Conan Doyle could add to the glamour of Sherlock Holmes by making him a drug addict—she presently reached out for a syringe and gave herself a shot of cocaine. 'I'm afraid I didn't act with much ginger tonight', she said.

While Tubby and the elder Miss May were engaged in gay dalliance on one sofa, she sitting beside me on another showed me her album, which contained many photographs of herself in many positions and circumstances, and numerous letters from excited admirers, some with signatures I knew. 'That was the only time I was *really* happy', she said, pointing to a photograph of herself in the bows of a white-sailed yacht.

But further confidences were interrupted by that most exhilarating of nineteenth century sounds—the galloping and clanging and shouting of the London fire brigade. We went to the tall windows. The sky was red with some not distant conflagration, and the cocaine having begun to work, Edna May proposed enthusiastically that we should go and watch it. We did from two hansoms—and for a long time. Then Tubby and I drove the ladies back again and went our several ways.

I did not have a good night. Now she was no longer present herself, the image of Edna May appeared before me with irresistible attractions. I determined to purchase the next day a splendid bouquet of various flowers, and meantime spent the small hours of the morning composing a poem in which each flower delivered its own message in turn. I can only recall one fragment of it:

> The Narcissus said my
> Gold little eye
> Will never gaze greedily;
> My petals are pale
> As a sunlit sail
> And my stalk is as green-as-the-sea.

And having composed these lines I lay with her in imagination and went to sleep.

SHOOTING WITH WILFRID BLUNT

1951

ILFRID BLUNT was almost the last host who ever asked
me down for a day's shooting. By the age of twenty-
five I had become the sort of young man no one could
possibly associate with sport; and I was not sorry. Why he
continued to ask me to shoot at Newbuildings, since I was so
poor a shot, I cannot guess—unless I was right when I sometimes
suspected that was a qualification in his eyes. It was for the
sake of his company and the sleeping beauty of his lovely small
old house that I invariably accepted, not for his birds.

Although winter afternoons were short, luncheon was always
leisurely and eaten in company with his Nurse. At table I
would produce any scraps of political or social gossip I had
brought down with me from London (he liked to be supplied
with it, though I was a disappointing gossip), and when my
little stock of news was out and he had made his comments,
we usually fell silent. Then, a white Arab mare with a fountain
tail would be brought to the steps from which the moss was
never scraped, and he would slowly swing himself into the
saddle, looking there I thought not unlike a photograph of the
old Count Tolstoy I had at home—only more handsome and
more worldly—but the poet—yes, very much the poet—obviously
enjoying the damp, still afternoon, the winter woods, and the
elastic paces of his mount.

Thus we would set off, I walking at one stirrup with my gun,
and a man-servant with a light bamboo chair over his arm at
the other, and a keeper and a few beaters following behind.
At the cover his chair would be placed at one spot while I was
stationed at another, to await that distant tapping which heralds
the rising of the birds. Then, my qualification, or disability, or
whatever you like to call it, came into play. With a startled

hiccup, a snapping of twigs, and whirring of wings a pheasant would presently fly out, followed by another and another. It was five to one (especially if they flew to the right of me) that I missed them. It was ten to one my host from his armchair brought them down: I think he enjoyed 'wiping my eye'. The bag was a matter of indifference. Once, at the close of such a day, he said: 'We may as well shoot two or three duck before we go in'; and off we went to a small pond on which a number of them were placidly swimming. It was not necessary to approach with caution, indeed they were hard to put up, being half tame. At last, after the manner of ducks, they began circling round and round their feeding-ground, ever higher and higher; and by a miracle my eye was in. Again and again as the flying wedge came over me, I pulled as by a string now a leader, now a straggler, out of the dusky sky. I was too excited and triumphant to notice that my host had stopped firing long ago. He was not pleased. He had meant the words 'two or three', and I had shot nearly a third of his carefully reared, hand-fed wild-duck! However, coals of fire were heaped on me next day in the shape of three brace in the railway-carriage rack above my head.

Wilfrid Blunt was suspicious of those in power (no one knew better how apt power is to make men stupid), and in his old age he was also jealous of the young. I am inclined to think that I owed his benevolence towards me partly to not being a shining specimen of youth. I was companionable without exciting envy. He used to say he detested young men; it would have been truer had he said they made him envious. He hated growing old. He never wrote more directly out of himself than in that fine sonnet which begins:

> I long have had a quarrel set with Time
> Because he robbed me. Every day of life
> Was wrested from me after bitter strife,
> I never yet could see the sun go down
> But I was angry in my heart.

Now, I was not the sort of young man who suggested successes in love, nor were my spirits of the towering sort. I could ride, play games, shoot after a fashion, but not with any skill that could remind him that his own heyday was over; and then, with reservations not hard to conceal, I admired him immensely. Admired? Well, it would perhaps be more accurate to say I relished him immensely: his personality, his bearded and bedouin handsomeness, his slightly daunting composure and good manners. No doubt he was vaguely aware that I did so, and more definitely that I appreciated enormously the beauty he had created round himself: Newbuildings Place was a house after my heart. Everything inside and out had been designed by one who knew that Time, the enemy, is also an artist. He understood the secret of creating habitable beauty: choose well, then let alone. I loved its dead-man's garden; and what would strike our plumber-pampered generation as its deplorable deficiencies were friendly features to me: in modern comforts I can find no dignity. I was attracted also by the freakish and fastidious collection of books the house contained, and by its pictures and the casual objects which lay about its tables. These, though often charming or curious in themselves, made you wonder first how they came there; they suggested stories.

Wilfrid Blunt was an aristocrat, and this, too, intrigued me. Already, even in my youth, aristocrats were becoming scarce enough, and I had met but a few. There was much in an aristocratic temper of mind which attracted and interested me. Many of the effects on character of pride still please me aesthetically; I like the indifference to appearances it breeds, combined with perfectly frank ostentation if occasion demands; I like its traditional hospitality; I like the confidence of manner, whether gentle or peremptory, which is a product of ancient riches. Aristocratic pride seems to me the best social substitute for magnanimity; and to one incorrigibly preoccupied with human nature it is also amusing to observe where, when real magnanimity is absent (which may be found in any walk of life), the make-shift may break down. An aristocrat can prove on occasion a dirty fighter—we all know that. You cannot behave like a cad and claim to be a gentleman, but a good deal of caddishness and the aristocratic temper have sometimes been compatible: Byron is a good example. Shorn of his privileges, the aristocrat may easily go considerable lengths in that direction partly because he feels deep down he has a right to his own way, and partly because his self-respect has no connection with what others think of him. It is tucked away with pride of birth in an odd corner of his mind, which private conscience may or may not visit, but social timidity never invades. Perhaps he feels that, with the exception of the scrupulous among them, those whom he considers equals will be likely to forgive him lack of delicacy before they pardon want of spirit. Meredith made a flashing study of such a type of person in the Earl of Fleetwood in *The Amazing Marriage*. It is getting rarer and rarer. It needs, if it is to flower with fine carelessness, to be surrounded by a wondering romantic sympathy tinged with awe; vague democratic snobbishness is not sustaining enough. A man cannot go on believing confidently that there is a subtle all-important difference between himself and common humanity without corroboration, and the climate of the twentieth century is unfavourable to that.

But I am digressing. Wilfrid Blunt did not afford an opportunity for observing the aristocrat as a dirty fighter. In political activities he was invariably on the side of the weak against the strong, of primitive civilisations against the Empire and commercialism. Like Byron he was on the side of the rebels —without democratic sympathies. His championship of causes —they were usually lost— was chivalrous. He was imprisoned by Arthur Balfour in Ireland for addressing a prohibited meeting, and he suffered acutely from cold in his cell and not being allowed to wear his top-coat. Shortly after his release, however, he had the pleasure of helping into it, at a tennis-party, the Irish Secretary who was at the moment afraid of catching a chill. It was the sort of small incident that Wilfrid Blunt enjoyed, and no doubt he accompanied the gesture with a few appropriate words. Both as fastidious aristocrat and poet, he loathed mechanism, commercialism, luxury, and fiddle-faddle democratic regulations. On the way from Three Bridges station to his other home, Crabbet Park, which before he died he handed over to his only child, Lady Wentworth, you passed a well surmounted by two notice-boards. The one declared in the name of the Local Authorities that the water was unsafe; the other, a more lengthy statement, asserted that it had been analysed by Savory and Moore and found drinkable—that was signed 'The Lord of the Manor'. Why shouldn't cottagers get their water from a source which they had always used? The retort of the Local Authorities was to board up the well; and there the two notices remained for years, getting more and more mud-bespattered, typical of the conflict between fading feudal paternalism and the machinery of modern governing bodies, ostensibly democratic but often with their own little axes to grind.

On his own estate, however, he knew how to create the spirit he desired. That spirit was legible in his plump, rosy-gilled garrulous agent, with his 'Yes, Squire', 'No, Squire', 'Certainly, Squire, O certainly'; in his wizened coachman, with a round, alarmed, bird-like eye, who on the box of a shabby old barouche, behind a pair of light and lovely Arab horses, met you at Horsham station; in (one surmised) his labourers and old gaffers who, certainly at one time, went about their work in smocks. At any rate nothing was run on the estate with a view to squeezing money out of it—if that was compensation for the domination of the Squire, who also sympathised with and respected every sort of rural craft and skill. William Morris, who reinforced his love of traditional country life and craftsmanship; the Arab, whose independence and personal dignity made the average English 'swell' seem like a genial, shoddy oaf —probably with one eye askew upon the main chance; and recollections of days when the aristocracy was in a much more confident position, were the chief elements in the preferences controlling his behaviour.

In that delightful book *The Theatre of Life*, Lord Howard of

Penrith recalls a Derby Day with him. There, every year, Blunt drove down a four-in-hand. This time he arrived too late to get to his place; whereupon he charged the police, galloped down the course, and swerved deftly into it. Towards the end of his life he was to drive a coach-and-four through conventions becoming to gentlemen; he published his Diaries in which he reported without scruple what friends had said of friends. There was an outcry; and one of them, looking back, has said with some truth, 'After all, it was Wilfrid Blunt who started the cad's chorus'.

Thus apart from their pleasantness, my visits gave me some insight into the effects of the aristocratic temper of mind on political opinions, country life, social life, and (but this requires separate treatment) on poetry. For Wilfrid Blunt, who remained an aristocrat when on the side of rebels, also remained one when writing poetry; he wore poetry like a ring on his finger. That is part of the charm of his verse.

Date Due